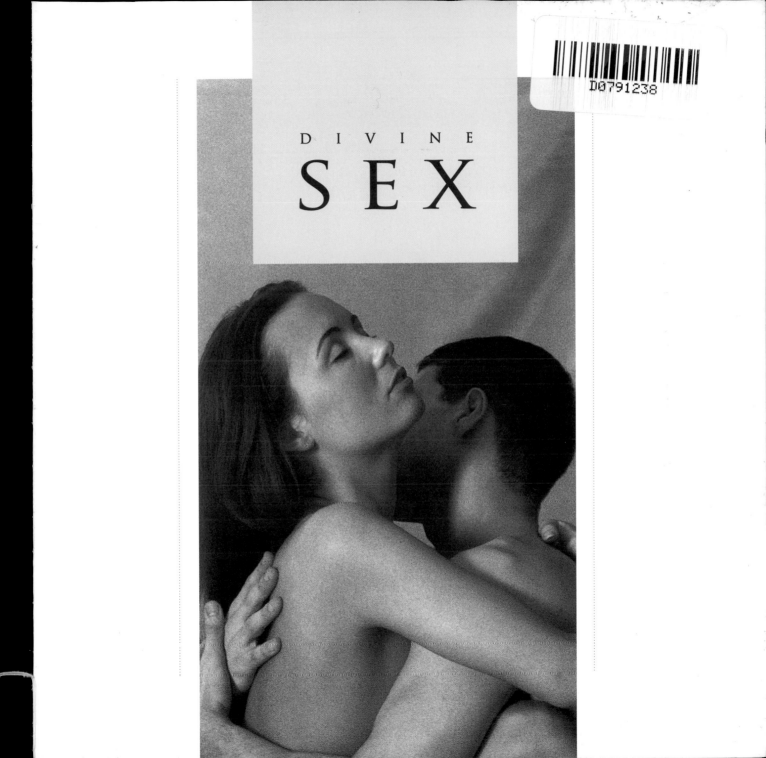

DIVINE
SEX

DIVINE
SEX

THE TANTRIC & TAOIST ARTS
OF CONSCIOUS LOVING

CAROLINE ALDRED

HarperSanFrancisco

An Imprint of HarperCollinsPublishers

Created and produced by
CARROLL & BROWN LIMITED
5 Lonsdale Road
London NW6 6RA

MANAGING EDITOR Denis Kennedy
ART DIRECTOR Chrissie Lloyd

PROJECT EDITOR Ian Wood
ART EDITOR Linley Clode
DESIGNER Susan Knight
PHOTOGRAPHY Debi Treloar
PRODUCTION Wendy Rogers Amanda Mackie

Divine Sex: *The Tantric and Taoist Arts of Conscious Loving.*

1

FIRST EDITION

Library of Congress Cataloging-in-Publication Data

Aldred, Caroline.
    Divine sex : the Tantric and Taoist arts of conscious loving/
Caroline Aldred. — 1st ed.
        p. cm.
    ISBN 0-06-251348-6 (pbk. : alk. paper)
    1. Sex instruction—Religious aspects—Tantrism. 2. Sex
instruction—Religious aspects—Taoism. 3. Sex—Religious aspects-
-Tantrism. 4. Sex—Religious aspects—Taoism. I. Title.
HQ64.A43 1996
613.9'6—dc20   95-33977
                                                            CIP

95 96 97 98 99 C&B 10 9 8 7 6 5 4 3 2 1

This edition is printed on acid-free paper that meets the
American National Standards Institute Z39.48 Standard.
Reproduced by Colourscan, Singapore

CONTENTS

INTRODUCTION 6

I TANTRA AND TAO 11

*Tantrism and Taoism • Harmony of Opposites
• Auras and Energies*

II THE BODY 25

*The Inner Man • The Inner Woman • Partner
and Principle • Sexual Anatomy • G-spot • Erogenous Zones
• Self-examination • Orgasm • Menstruation*

III YOGA 47

*Stamina and Suppleness • Diet • Breathing Exercises
• Bodily Fitness and Yoga*

IV MIND AND SPIRIT 81

Meditation • Reflexology • Awakening the Senses

V PREPARING FOR LOVE 91

*Rituals • Seeing the God and Goddess in Each Other
• Body Ornamentation • Creating the Mood • Massage
• Foreplay • Oral Sex • Homosexuality • The Forbiddens*

VI LOVEMAKING 117

*Basic and Advanced Postures • Channeling Energy
• Mutual Absorption • Afterplay*

VII SEXUAL HEALING 139

Sexual Health • Healing Postures • Safer Sex

GLOSSARY 154 • INDEX 156 • FURTHER READING 160

INTRODUCTION

Sex is a subject that immediately demands attention, and it is a subject that I am passionate about and fascinated by—and it seems I am not alone! Sex permeates every cell of our bodies, and is our most potent creative energy. It touches and inspires every aspect of our lives, and it affects us emotionally, physically, and spiritually.

CROWN CHAKRA
The crown chakra, represented by a lotus flower with a thousand petals, is one of the seven energy centers in the subtle body.

Sex is also a natural source of pleasure with the potential to move beyond the purely physical into an experience of egolessness, timelessness, and oneness with the universe. Good sex promotes a healthy, happy, and potentially divine experience of life on every level, and the sexual secrets of the ancient Eastern philosophies of Tantrism and Taoism can be applied and adapted to suit our modern lives. They offer us a different perspective on the art of lovemaking, the healing benefits of sex, and the cultivation and transmutation of sexual energy into expanded consciousness and a longer, happier, wiser, and more spiritual life.

My own discovery of the spirituality of sex began in London in the mid-eighties when, at the suggestion of a lover and in between acting jobs, I started studying T'ai Chi Chuan, the traditional Chinese art of meditative exercise. Through this, I began to experience my body and my "self" in a way that was totally new to me. Emotions were triggered, my physical body was changing, and I felt "connected". It was the beginning of a journey into an aspect of myself that had, as yet, found no expression. The journey continued soon after when I met a Tantric Yogi, who was visiting London from Bali.

At that time, I knew nothing about Tantra except that it had originated in India and thought it had something to do with sex. But I quickly became interested in it when its scope and depth had been explained to me, and for the next five years I studied different aspects of Tantra. I soon learned that sex is only one, comparatively small, aspect of Tantra.

The origins of Tantra are obscure and probably will never be known, but they certainly long predate the oldest Tantric texts, which are thought to date from no earlier than A.D. 400–600. Tantra has its roots in Hinduism, and is a combination of art, science, and religion that requires of its followers the knowledge and understanding of a range of subjects including yoga, breath control, meditation, mantra, yantra, and ritual.

Acquiring this knowledge serves as preparation for initiation into the secrets of sexual union, which, as I had known earlier, is an important aspect of Tantra. Ajit Mookerjee and Madhu Khanna

in The Tantric Way *describe Tantra from the point of view of "expansion", thus: "Tantra means knowledge of a systematic and scientific experimental method which offers the possibility of expanding man's consciousness and faculties, a process through which the individual's inherent spiritual powers can be realized." Tantra is about accepting yourself as you are, not fighting with yourself and not resisting your natural instincts. This includes accepting that sex is natural and vital to our existence, and that as an energy it has as much importance and relevance to everyday life as breathing or any other bodily function.*

YANTRA
A yantra is a mystical diagram that can be used as an aid to meditation. This one symbolizes the goddess Kali.

The practices of Tantra, and those of the ancient Chinese Taoist tradition, provide practical means of acquiring a deep understanding of sexual love, so enhancing the experience, strengthening the bonds of love and trust between the two partners, and balancing and harmonizing the male and female energies. Sexual union is used as a way of uniting the spirit with the flesh, and by this means we can experience the unlimited potential of our spiritual powers and the inherent divinity within each of us.

For those who are responsible seekers of knowledge, and who have the desire to integrate their sexuality with their spirituality, the Tantric and Taoist practices of sexual love provide the methods and techniques necessary for a deeper understanding. They lead to a reconnection with one's original identity and with the source of the universe through the acceptance and utilization of our human desires and feelings. This is accompanied by an expansion of consciousness and the potential for self-realization through which personal liberation and the full development of one's spiritual powers may be achieved within a single lifetime.

Taoism, like Tantra, is an ancient body of knowledge dating back many thousands of years, and it is a complete system of living. According to Dr. Stephen Chang, in his book The Tao of Sexology, *it comprises eight disciplines of personal cultivation, known collectively as The Eight Pillars of Taoism, which are: The Tao of Philosophy; The Tao of Revitalization; The Tao of Balanced Diet; The Tao of the Forgotten Food Diet; The Tao of Healing Art; The Tao of Sex Wisdom; The Tao of Mastery; and The Tao of Success.*

FIVE ESSENTIALS
This diagram symbolizes the goddess Shakti and the Rite of Five Essentials.

The Tao of Sex Wisdom, or The Tao of Loving, is sex that is taught and practiced in accordance with the other seven disciplines of Taoism. Its objective is for men and women to achieve the fundamental harmony of Yin and Yang—the two opposing but complementary aspects or energies of the universe—by cultivating sexual energy and using sex as a means of improving and maintaining health and increasing spirituality. The interaction of Yin and Yang, which is the source of all life, is the foundation of Taoist philosophy. Earth is the Yin, or female aspect, and heaven the Yang, or male. By harmoniously balancing within ourselves the energy of heaven with that of earth, harmony in other areas of life will follow. The dance between Yin and Yang constitutes the whole, just as the joining of man and woman creates a unity in which both partners benefit from each other's essence and combine in harmony.

Early Taoist physicians recognized lovemaking as a part of the natural order of things and considered it necessary to the physical and mental well-being of men and women. Love and sex were considered an important part of Chinese medicine, which advocated using sex and sexual energy for improving health, harmonizing relationships, and increasing spiritual realization. The Taoist practices teach us how to cultivate life force, or chi. *They focus on integrating the subtle energies in the body to achieve the balance of Yin and Yang, and the attraction between the two and the potency of sexual energy is the key.*

YOGA
Meditation and yoga help to prepare the mind and body for Tantric lovemaking.

The basic principles of The Tao of Loving are the control and regulation of male ejaculation and the importance of female satisfaction. Taoists believe that sex is only beneficial when it is totally satisfying, and then it is considered of great benefit to both partners. In Taoist sexual practice, the man learns how to experience orgasms without ejaculation. By retaining his semen instead of ejaculating, the man strengthens his physical body, conserving his vital energy or life force. This allows him to make love as often—and for as long—as both partners wish, or for as long as it takes for his partner to achieve complete satisfaction.

I hope this book will appeal to people who recognize the sacredness of sex, and to those of you who wish to experiment with and to experience the creative and healing potential of lovemaking.

LOVEMAKING
The Tantric and Taoist techniques of lovemaking help to ensure ecstasy and true satisfaction for both partners.

Tantrism and Taoism both offer practical methods of lovemaking that transcend the purely physical, but the only way that you can experience the benefits of these ancient and highly effective techniques is to practice them. They are described here in a very straightforward form to spark your interest and inspire you to try them and integrate them into your daily life. I hope that they also promote an understanding of the "self," so that physical union with your partner can become an experience of ecstatic bliss in which your sexual energy moves upward to be transformed into spiritual energy.

Caroline Forbes

I

TANTRA
AND TAO

TANTRISM AND TAOISM

The principles of two ancient Eastern philosophies, Tantrism and Taoism, are becoming increasingly popular in the West, particularly with those who wish to integrate their sexuality with their spiritual growth. Both doctrines recognize that our sexual energy is our most potent creative force and that individual self-enlightenment can be obtained by cultivating and utilizing this energy.

Tantric teachings evolved in India and then spread to Tibet, China, Nepal, Japan, and Southeast Asia. It is not known exactly when they were first introduced, but there are Tantric texts that can be dated to A.D. 400–600. Tantra provides practical methods of developing a total awareness of your physical potential, plus acceptance of all emotions, sensations, and desires, so that you can face and transcend the polar opposites of pain and pleasure, destruction and creativity, and darkness and light.

> **"Woman is the living body, man is the living mind, and beyond the two exists living spirit."** OSHO

Taoism is an ancient philosophy from China. It is considered to be one of the oldest sciences of life, and is a system of knowledge and practice that embraces many principles, including physical exercise, food and diet, healing, and sexology. The goal of Taoism is for the individual to acquire and maintain as much inner energy as possible.

Although there are many similarities between the Taoist and Tantric approaches to sex, one crucial difference is that the Taoist approach is based on medicine, while that of Tantra is rooted in religion. For both, however, liberation of the entire being is the goal.

TANTRA

The word "Tantra" is a Sanskrit word that can be translated as "weaving" or "expansion," and Tantrism is a philosophy and way of life that includes the conscious and creative utilization of sexual energy to achieve liberation from the limits of the individual self. This liberation heightens awareness of the bliss and joy of each moment, not just in sex but in all of life, and engenders what yoga teacher and author James Hewitt describes as "an exuberant 'yes-saying' to the experiences of living." Tantric practices take many forms, including the repetition of *mantras* (mystical sounds and words) and the study of *yantras* (symbolic geometric forms that represent the different forces of energy).

They also include the worship and invocation of deities, ritual practices, yoga, and various visualization and meditational techniques. These practices are intended to awaken the senses and create physical, mental, and psychic stimulation that will lead to enlightenment and an understanding of the indivisible unity of all things.

Tantrists regard sexual union, *maithuna*, as a rite aimed at using physical love to awaken *kundalini* (the latent energy at the base of the spine) and direct it upward through the *chakras* (energy centers) in the psychic body to the crown of the head. This creates a state of spiritual ecstasy.

THE TAO

The word "Tao" means "the way," and refers to the way of the universe and the awareness of physical and nonphysical existence. For thousands of years, the aim of Taoist sages has been to achieve a state of "oneness" with the Tao, which is everywhere and nowhere at the same time and cannot be seen or felt, but which permeates everything. The Taoists were close observers of nature and they believed that to be natural—in harmony with the forces and balance of nature—was essential for the cultivation and direction of inner energy to promote health, longevity, and spiritual fulfilment.

The practices of Taoism were kept secret from the masses and originally revealed only to Taoist scholars and the emperors. The secrets were passed down orally for thousands of years, and the first written account of the basic principles of Taoism was probably the *Tao Te Ching*. This text, which is about 5,000 words long and divided into two books, is traditionally attributed to a sage called Lao Tzu and appeared some time before the end of the fourth century B.C., perhaps as early as the sixth century.

From the earliest days, one of the central tenets of Taoism was the importance of an energetic and happy sex life, and the production of detailed and explicit Taoist sexological texts date from over 2,000 years ago up to the present day.

These provide a wealth of information on sexual technique, the aim of which is the achievement of tranquility and health through the harmony of *Yin* (female) and *Yang* (male). This harmony can be attained by ensuring female satisfaction through male self-control.

One of the first Taoist sex manuals, and still one of the best, was the *Su Nü Ching (The Classic of the Plain Girl),* which was written in the second or third century B.C. This relates the advice given to the Yellow Emperor (Huang Ti) by his three female sexual advisors—Su Nü (the Plain Girl), Hsüan Nü (the Mysterious Girl), and Tsai Nü (the Rainbow Girl).

THE HARMONY OF OPPOSITES

In Tantrism, the deities Shiva and Shakti represent the two opposing forces of masculine and feminine, positive and negative. Shiva is the male principle, his consort, Shakti, is the female principle, and the sexual union of man and woman represents the union of Shiva and Shakti. In Taoism, the two opposing forces are represented by Yin and Yang.

SHIVA

In the Hindu tradition from which Tantra sprang, Shiva is sometimes regarded as one of the three aspects of the Supreme Being: Brahma, the creator, Vishnu, the preserver, and Shiva, the destroyer. In this context, destruction implies subsequent renewal—Shiva is also the reproductive power that restores and regenerates, and that is why he is often symbolized by a *lingam,* or phallus. In Tantric belief, Shiva pulls from the heavens while Shakti pushes up from the earth. They have a mutual attraction and the eternal play between them—the Dance of Shiva and Shakti— makes up the universe as we know it.

SHAKTI

Shakti, who is often symbolized by a *yoni,* or vulva, is worshipped in many forms including that of Devi, the mother goddess. Devi herself can take on different forms, either gentle (such as Uma and Gauri) or fierce (such as Kali and Durga). Both Shiva and Shakti reside within us, each in an energy center, or *chakra* (see page 18). Shakti resides in the base chakra, centered on the perineum, and Shiva in the crown chakra at the top of the head, and when they are brought together in harmony, the veil of illusion (*Maya,* the manifest universe, where consciousness is buried) is lifted and liberation is attained.

YIN AND YANG

Like the Tantrists, the Taoists believe that all existence evolves from the interaction of two opposing but complementary forces or energies. In the Taoist tradition, these two forces are known as Yin and Yang, and the constant interplay between them makes up the entire universe. When a correct balance of the two eternal opposites is achieved, they are mutually interdependent and permeate each other, creating harmony.

The Taoists perceive the universe as constantly altering, and believe that the best, most natural course of action for a person to follow in any particular situation is the one that is the most closely attuned to the underlying cosmic harmony or universal pattern.

The principles of Yin and Yang still underpin many aspects of Chinese culture, just as they have done for thousands of years. Much of Chinese medicine, for example, is based on achieving a proper balance between the two.

SEX AND SYMBOLISM

In Taoism, the sexual union of man and woman symbolizes the union of Yin and Yang, of heaven and earth. According to the *I Ching* (the *Book of Changes*), which was probably written in the thirteenth century B.C., "The eternal intermingling of Heaven and Earth gives form to all things, and the sexual union of male and female gives life to all things."

Yin is the Cosmic Feminine, symbolized by woman, water, and earth. It is seen as being receptive, inward-moving, dark, yielding, weak, soft, passive, and changeable. Yang, the Cosmic Masculine, is symbolized by man, fire, and heaven. In contrast to Yin, Yang is resistant, outward-moving, light, hard, and active, and it is considered the primary force that binds the whole of the universe together. Man and woman each embody the qualities of both Yin and Yang, and it is the predominance of one or the other that determines the gender of the individual.

THE YIN/YANG SYMBOL

The traditional circular symbol that represents the union of Yin and Yang is familiar to most people, even if they are unaware of its significance. The symbol represents the Supreme Source, and consists of a circle divided into two by a curved boundary that separates the Yin (black) from the Yang (white). The smooth curvature of this boundary signifies that the balance between Yin and Yang is never fixed, and each half of the symbol contains within it a dot of its opposite principle.

YIN/YANG SYMBOL
The symbol represents the polar opposites, Yin and Yang, which together make up the whole. Each is balanced by and contained within the other. Their mutual attraction and their interaction creates movement, change, and a flow of energy or life force, known as chi.

AURAS AND ENERGIES

Hindus and Tantrists consider that a living being is made up of three main elements: the physical body; the self or spirit; and the subtle body. The subtle body is the nonphysical body that is believed to connect this world with the next. The energizing effects of yoga (see page 48) and Pranayama exercises (see page 54) intensify and activate the subtle body.

THE SUBTLE BODY

The subtle body surrounds and permeates the physical body, and manifests itself outside it as an energy field, or aura. Some people with psychic powers can see or sense the aura surrounding a person, and the technique of Kirlian photography (invented in Russia by Semyon Kirlian) produces images thought to represent it.

The subtle body is made up of energy centers, or chakras (see page 18), and channels, called *nadis,* through which energy flows. The chakras are points of contact between the subtle and physical body; nadis are rooted in the base chakra *(Muladhara)* and form an intricate network extending through the entire subtle body.

PRANA, CHI, AND CHING

Central to Tantric and Taoist philosophies is the idea of a subtle form of energy that is carried in the atmosphere and animates all forms of matter, including humans. In Tantric belief, this energy, known as *prana,* flows through the nadis in the subtle body. Pranayama, one of the forms of yoga, teaches how to control prana and store it in the body by using breath control. The movement and conservation of prana through yoga and pranayama brings strength, vitality, and nourishment to different parts of the body.

> **"When the kundalini is sleeping it will be aroused by the grace of the guru."**
>
> SWAMI SVATMARAMA

To the Taoists, the subtle energy is known as *chi,* and is the invisible energy that we "feel" in our bodies. It binds the physical and metaphysical bodies, and the interplay of positively and negatively charged chi energies keeps our hearts pumping and our minds dreaming, and is responsible for our emotions.

Ancient Taoist masters, living in and with nature, noticed the flow of chi through everything, pervading the whole universe, and developed ways of cultivating and utilizing the flow of chi within their bodies, thus achieving a balance and harmony that brought them physical health, longevity, and spirituality. As far as possible, this balance needs to come from within, but balance is also created when you join with another of the opposite sex because then you are exchanging energies and circulating energy between you.

The basic energy within the body, and the source of all our energy, is raw chi that has been transformed by the body into a more potent form—sexual energy, or *ching*. This is stored in the body, and when it stops flowing, you die. It has the power of procreation and can also be transformed into spiritual energy.

In its physical form, ching is stored in the sperm and ovaries. When you feel sexually aroused you are experiencing an expansion of your ching essence and your whole being is charged with new energy.

NADIS

There are believed to be over 70,000 nadis in the subtle body. The principal nadi, the Sushumna, is a vertical column that corresponds to the spinal cord and connects the seven main chakras. Spiralling around the Sushumna are two other important nadis, the Ida and the Pingala. These two channels control feminine and masculine energy: Ida represents the lunar aspect, which is feminine, and Pingala represents the solar aspect, which is masculine.

Ida originates at the left side of the base chakra and spirals up and around the Sushumna to the right nostril. Pingala has its origin at the right side of the base chakra and it spirals up the Sushumna to the left nostril.

VITAL AIRS
Prana is just one of ten energies or "vital airs" that flow through the nadis, another being *apana*. Prana moves upward and apana downward, and when both unite in the base chakra, the dormant energy, kundalini, is aroused (see page 20).

The yoga technique of *Anuloma viloma*, or Alternate Nostril Breathing (see page 56) is a means of stimulating the activity of both Ida and Pingala: the left nostril is considered to be the path of Ida, and the right nostril the path of Pingala. This breathing exercise ensures that there is an equal flow of prana through and around each side of the body, which helps to balance the left ("verbal") and right ("visual") hemispheres of the brain.

Pingala

Sushumna

Ida

IDA, PINGALA, AND SUSHUMNA
The most important of the subtle body's 70,000 nadis are the Sushumna, and the Ida and Pingala which spiral around it.

CHAKRAS

The chakras (Sanskrit for "wheels") are vortices of energy that connect the subtle body with the physical body. There are seven main chakras, which are located at the base of the spine, the lower abdomen, solar plexus, heart, throat, forehead, and above the crown of the head.

Chakras are visualized and depicted as lotus flowers, each petal of which symbolizes the blossoming of a quality or mental attribute. Each chakra is associated with a particular psychological or spiritual function, such as creativity or sexuality, and most are also associated with an element, such as air or fire. With the exception of the crown chakra, each has its own mantra, a vocalized meditational sound (see page 21) that resonates with the natural vibrations of that individual chakra.

Chakras can be either open or closed, and may be activated by techniques including yoga, meditation, and lovemaking. When kundalini energy (see page 20) is stirred, it travels up through the subtle body, stimulating each chakra in turn to open. It then absorbs each chakra's energy, leaving it closed, until it reaches the crown and merges with cosmic consciousness.

DISCOVERING YOUR CHAKRAS

To attune yourself to your chakras, locate the site of each one in turn and then imagine it superimposed onto your physical body. Starting at the base chakra, work upward and visualize the appropriate color at each region of your body. When you visualize each chakra, repeatedly intone its mantra (see opposite). Inhale between each intonation, visualizing your breath filling the chakra; its color may grow brighter and stronger as its lotus petals unfold.

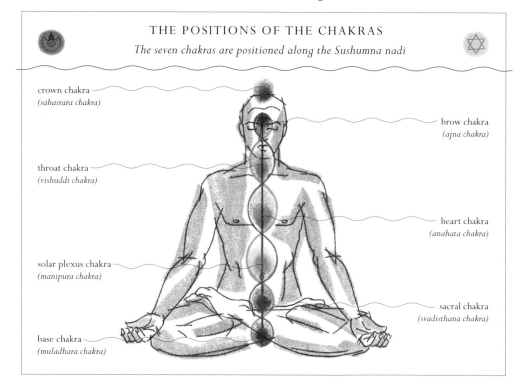

THE POSITIONS OF THE CHAKRAS

The seven chakras are positioned along the Sushumna nadi

crown chakra
(sahasrara chakra)

brow chakra
(ajna chakra)

throat chakra
(vishuddi chakra)

heart chakra
(anahata chakra)

solar plexus chakra
(manipura chakra)

sacral chakra
(svadisthana chakra)

base chakra
(muladhara chakra)

CROWN CHAKRA
color: **violet**
mantra: **none**
petals: **1,000**
element: **none**
location: **crown of head**
function: **union, wisdom**

BROW CHAKRA
color: **indigo**
mantra: **OM**
petals: **2**
element: **none**
location: **brow**
function: **perception**

THROAT CHAKRA
color: **bright blue**
mantra: **HAM**
petals: **16**
element: **akasa
(ether/space)**
location: **throat**
function: **creativity**

HEART CHAKRA
color: **green**
mantra: **YAM**
petals: **12**
element: **air**
location: **heart**
function: **love**

SOLAR PLEXUS CHAKRA
color: **yellow**
mantra: **RAM**
petals: **10**
element: **fire**
location: **solar plexus**
function: **power, will**

SACRAL CHAKRA
color: **orange**
mantra: **VAM**
petals: **6**
element: **water**
location: **sacral plexus**
function: **sexuality, pleasure**

BASE CHAKRA
color: **red**
mantra: **LAM**
petals: **4**
element: **earth**
location: **perineum**
function: **survival, grounding**

KUNDALINI

Kundalini is the all-powerful but normally latent female energy located in the base chakra (Muladhara) at the lower end of the Sushumna nadi. The name is Sanskrit for "coiled up," and kundalini is traditionally depicted as a dormant serpent coiled three and a half times, sometimes with its tail in its mouth.

Also known as Kundalini Shakti or "inner woman," kundalini exists in every human being, but may lie dormant and unnoticed throughout one's lifetime. Once she is awakened, however, the experience is dramatic. It has been likened to a rush of intense heat through the body that brings with it a feeling of giddiness. Sometimes, you will also tremble, your breathing may become spasmodic, and you might hear inner sounds and feel a sense of colors, shapes and patterns dissolving into an intensely radiant pure light. It is an energy so powerful that it can change your life forever.

The Tantric practice of kundalini yoga is aimed at awakening and channeling this dormant energy so that it travels upward from the base chakra, which is the abode of Shakti, to the crown chakra (sahasrara), where Shiva lives. This unites Shakti (the universe) with Shiva (pure consciousness),

AROUSING THE COILED SERPENT
Kundalini energy is usually depicted as a coiled serpent, which lies dormant at the base of the Sushumna nadi. During lovemaking, the physical movements in the sexual region— combined with deep breathing, positive visualization, and the sounds of love—can awaken kundalini and elevate physical love to a mystical dimension of timelessness and oneness with the universe.

a mystical union that leads to personal liberation or enlightenment.

As the kundalini energy is stirred and travels upward, it passes through each chakra in turn and awakens its energies. This allows the individual to experience higher and higher states of consciousness, and eventually attain a state of pure bliss.

Because kundalini energy is so powerful it can act destructively as well as creatively, and in order to avoid the destructive side of its nature, yogis go through years of training and discipline when preparing for its release. This preparation involves techniques such as physical and breathing exercises, meditation, and dietary control. These prepare the physical and subtle bodies for kundalini's release by helping to clear blockages so that the aroused energy can move unhindered through the chakras to the crown. But the yogic methods are not the only way to awaken kundalini energy: music, dance, and lovemaking also can arouse it. By using Tantric lovemaking techniques, couples can learn how to channel this energy, and by using the serpent power as a creative ally, they can experience blissful ecstasy beyond the realms of normal consciousness.

Mantras

The universe is made up of sound, and each sound is a form of energy that has a unique vibrational quality. Mantras are syllables or phrases, composed of consonants and vowels, that are considered to have particularly potent vibrational qualities. They are powerful tools for meditation (see page 84), and traditionally they are received from a guru, or teacher.

There are many different kinds of mantra, all of which can be repeated out loud, whispered, or spoken silently in your head—even unconsciously. For example, each time we breathe we unconsciously repeat a mantra—"so" on the in breath and "ham" on the out breath. This translates as "I am that I am."

When a mantra is repeated out loud, its rhythm and vibration help us to ward off disturbing negative thoughts, and the release of the sound's energy creates a specific positive thought pattern. Thus mantras are a method for sending out our own good vibrations to counter any disharmonious ones. They give us power to take control of our minds and bodies.

The power of a mantra is experienced through its use. This power is subtle and you need to allow yourself time to experience its effectiveness. Probably the best known mantra is "Om." It is said to be the original sound from which the universe was created—the root of all sounds. The sound is made up of three different parts—AH...OO...MM—and careful pronunciation is important. Whether intoned vocally or practiced inwardly, "AH" is generated from deep within the body, "OO" is short, and "MM," which is the longest sound, resonates through the head.

Reciting a mantra can be a useful aid to meditation, but you should choose your mantra carefully. Try out different sounds or phrases, either known or made up, or use a positive affirmation about yourself.

OM
The Sanskrit characters for the mantra "Om."

MANTRAS AND MEDITATION
For thousands of years, students of yoga have used mantras as an aid to meditation.

Repeat it for 10 or 20 minutes or so, verbally or internally, as a means of focusing your mind.

You can also use mantras during lovemaking, to help you concentrate your mind and control your sexual energy, and keep you "in the moment."

YANTRAS

In Eastern teaching and studies, sound and form are interrelated: every sound has a visual equivalent, which represents the the shape of the sound, and mantras (see page 21) are represented by geometric patterns known as yantras. These carefully constructed mystical diagrams are used as aids to meditation.

THE STRUCTURE OF A YANTRA

The geometry of yantra designs is intended to help the meditator focus his or her mind and turn awareness inward. Many classic yantras are also designed to capture potent energy patterns that represent specific deities, such as Kali and Tara.

Because it is a visual pattern, contemplating a yantra involves using the right hemisphere of the brain, the "visual" side that is concerned with the recognition and memory of shapes and also with concrete thinking and emotions. A mantra, being a sound, activates the left hemisphere of the brain, which is the "verbal" side that deals with speech and abstract thinking.

When a meditator combines the contemplation of a yantra with the recitation of a suitable mantra, he or she is actively involving both brain hemispheres in the act of meditation. With both sides of the brain acting in harmony, the meditator is able to reach a higher state of awareness and feel at one with the universe.

The drawing and coloring of a yantra, which was traditionally done according to strict rules that governed such factors as the type of brushes and inks to use, is also an act of meditation utilizing both sides of the brain. Drawing the geometric outlines involves the right side, and adding the colors, the left. The Sanskrit word "yantra" may be translated simply as "tool," but it can also signify something that liberates. There are many varieties of yantra, some of the most important being the *Shakta Yantras* that represent manifestations of the Divine Mother.

The basic format of these yantras consists of a square frame with a T-shaped projection on each of its sides. Inside the square, two or more concentric circles contain a ring of lotus petals, and within the innermost circle a pattern of one or more triangles encloses the central point, or *bindu,* of the yantra. Each of these

TARA YANTRA
This yantra symbolizes the goddess Tara, one of the forms of the Divine Mother. The yantra has an eight-petalled lotus, signifying the physical world, and its focal point, the bindu, is contained within an upward-pointing triangle.

geometric elements, such as squares, circles, and triangles, has its own particular symbolism, as do the many other shapes used in the design of yantras.

SQUARES, CIRCLES, AND POINTS

The square provides a foundation and framework for the other design elements of a yantra, supporting and containing them without intruding upon them. The T-shaped projections on each side of a yantra square represent gateways.

The bindu, the dot at the centre of a yantra, is the focal point of the whole diagram. It represents the male seed, the source of all creation, the supreme consciousness, and the most condensed form of energy, and although the bindu has location it has no magnitude.

A circle, which in geometrical terms can be defined as the symmetrical expansion of a point, represents the cyclic forces of the universe and its continual renewal, and also space and infinity. A series of three concentric circles can represent the three qualities of energy, or *Gunas* (see page 50). Three such circles can also symbolize past, present, and future, the three inseparable aspects of time.

TRIANGLES, STARS, AND PETALS

The triangle is one of the most important of the basic geometric symbols used in yantras. When it points up, it represents upward movement and male energy, and when it points down, it symbolizes downward movement, female energy, and the yoni (vulva).

When these two triangles are combined, they make a six-pointed star that denotes a harmonious balance of male and female energies. The concept of balance can also be signified by an eight-pointed star created by superimposing one square on top of another.

One of the most potent yantra symbols consists of a downward-pointing triangle, symbolizing the yoni and surrounding a central point, which represents the male seed. Together, they are symbolic of the continuing existence of the world through a process of continuous creation.

Lotus petals are another common motif in yantra design, and are usually depicted in a ring. The meaning of a ring of lotus petals in a yantra depends on the number of petals that are depicted: eight petals signify manifest reality, 12 denote the sun, and 16 the moon.

KALI YANTRA
The yantra of the goddess Kali contains three concentric circles and three triangles. In this yantra, the concentric circles represent the three aspects of time, and the triangles are used to symbolize the three Gunas.

MANDALAS

A *mandala* is a mystical diagram, a circular image signifying wholeness and totality, an expression of the psychological processes of unfolding and integration. Well-known examples of mandalas include the symbol of Yin and Yang (see page 15), and the round windows often found in churches and temples. Mandalas, yantras, and deities comprise the mainstream of Tantric art and are widely used in Tantric ritual.

TIBETAN MANDALA
A mandala is a mystical diagram or an energy pattern that is used as a meditation symbol.

THE STRUCTURE OF A MANDALA

The word "mandala" is Sanskrit for "circle," and this reflects the traditional circular shape of these complex and subtle designs. According to *Mystery of Mandalas,* by Heita Copony, "There are three principles of order in the structure of a mandala: the center; emanations radiating from the center; and the periphery of the circle. So a mandala is concentrated on its central point, the birthplace of all existence in space and time, from which all movement emanates and to which everything leads."

The Tantric author, Ajit Mookerjee, describes a mandala as representing the cosmos, whose beginning is in its end, and whose end is in its beginning. He also describes Tantric adepts as being "trained to visualize the primal essence of the mandala in its external form and then to internalize it, through contemplation, into a psychic force."

Ritual mandalas, especially those of the classical Tibetan tradition, are composed of very detailed and complex patterns and symbols, and are restricted to a formal structure of defined styles and motifs. Mandalas are usually painted (typically in gouache) on cloth or paper, and the process of drawing the mandala is considered in itself to be a meditation.

TRADITIONAL FORMS

In classical Tantric art, the mandala artist had to practice complex visual formulation, probably from an early age, in order to be able to evoke the universe and draw the divine and cosmic symbols accurately. He had to comply strictly with the traditional forms, using an established range of precisely prescribed symbols, shapes, and colors to transmit eternal spiritual truths and spiritual power to any person who was contemplating or meditating on the mandala.

MANDALAS AND MEDITATION

By meditating on a mandala, the experienced meditator is able to concentrate cosmic and psychic energy. The image portrayed reflects the inner self, and by contemplating the mandala and its meaning, as Heita Copony writes, "meditators become aware of their own complex multidimensional existence…the nature of birth and death, and the unalterable oneness of all being."

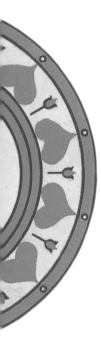

II

THE BODY

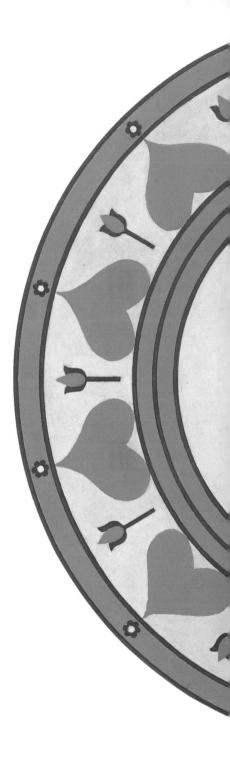

EXPLORING SEXUALITY

To be able to reach the heights of sexual ecstasy with your partner, you need to be aware of your own body and its potential for sexuality. You also have to get to know your partner's body, its sexual anatomy, and its response to sexual stimulation.

We all differ in our sexual responses just as much as we do in our physical and emotional characteristics. Exploring your sexuality and discovering your individual pattern of sexual responses will not only provide you with self-knowledge, it will also give you more sexual self-confidence. As well as getting to know your own sexual responses, you should learn those of your partner and find out how he or she likes to be touched, caressed, kissed, and stimulated. By doing so, you will be better able to help maximize your partner's pleasure during lovemaking, especially when you know his or her sexual preferences so well that providing optimum stimulation becomes almost intuitive.

> **"Yang functions only with the cooperation of Yin; Yin can grow only in the presence of Yang."**
> LAO TZU

MUSCLE CONTROL
Another way to increase your own sexual pleasure and that of your partner is to learn how to control the muscles of your genital region, especially your pelvic floor (pubococcygeal, or PC) muscles. In a woman, tensing these muscles tightens the grip of the vagina on the penis during intercourse, increasing her pleasure and that of her partner (see page 32). In a man, being able to control the pelvic floor muscles (see page 43) contributes to overall genital fitness and, more importantly, helps him to control ejaculation.

EJACULATION CONTROL
In Tantric and Taoist sexology, ejaculation control and semen retention are among the most important sexual skills that a man can develop. These skills help him to achieve orgasm without ejaculation, preserving his Yang essence and enabling him to prolong intercourse and ensure that his partner has the opportunity to reach the highest levels of sexual ecstasy.

Other techniques that a couple can use to enhance sexual pleasure include stimulation of the woman's G-spot (see page 29) and of the man's prostate gland (see page 39). The G-spot can be stimulated either manually or, during intercourse, with the penis, and the prostate gland is easily stimulated with a finger.

Inner Man, Inner Woman

To transform sexual energy into healing and spiritual energy, both partners must be committed to moving beyond personality and ego, finding the correct balance of Yin and Yang, and keeping the flow of these energies harmonious. It is important that each partner develops an ability to know, understand, and "feel" the energy of the other, and to give and receive openly and willingly. A crucial part of this ability is the recognition that essentially we are all bisexual. By this I mean that each man is both male and female and each woman is both female and male.

MASCULINE AND FEMININE ASPECTS

Man is associated with fire and masculine energy, or Yang energy, a dynamic, active energy that, whatever our gender, we all have within us. "Masculine" qualities are those of intellect, ambition, and assertiveness, which are translated into male characteristics. Woman is associated with water, and femininity with intuitive, passive, free-flowing energy, the Yin aspect of everyone's nature. "Feminine" qualities are those of nurturing, receptivity, and caring.

We need to find the balance of these two aspects without repression or fear. Being vulnerable can be an expression of strength in men, and for women there is great power in being assertive while maintaining femininity. From an early age, physical gender affects our behaviour patterns, often repressing these natural, secondary, yet evident male or female aspects of our personalities. So as men and women we should feel free to exercise and recognize the functioning of the male and female aspects within ourselves.

If we open ourselves to embracing the different qualities of our feminine and masculine sides we become more balanced and complete human beings, and are able to develop a greater and deeper understanding of our partners. And being aware of our new-found "selves" imparts a sense of confidence that is always attractive.

Men and women are undeniably different, but this difference should find expression not as competition or power but revolve around balance. Finding this balance begins inside ourselves, where within one body both sexes are embraced in the divine union of Shiva and Shakti, of Yin and Yang. When lovemaking becomes a Tantric ritual, the woman is the doorway for the man to experience his inner woman and the man awakens his partner to the presence of her inner man.

There is great value to be gained from exchanging roles during lovemaking: you play out and express your feminine aspect if you are a man, and your masculine aspect if you are a woman. Each of you offers a perfect reflection of the other's inner aspects, so when you explore these during lovemaking it creates an exchange of energy, passive and active in perfect harmony and not limited by gender.

THE FEMALE PARTNER

I hope that both men and women will read the following pages, because it is important that both sexes understand each other's bodies and their responses to sexual arousal.

The physical differences between men and women have an effect on their psychological and spiritual development, so gaining a clear understanding of how the male and female bodies function is an important step toward understanding the humanness of each other.

The human body is nothing to be ashamed of: rather it is something to celebrate, and the flesh and the spirit are one in the eyes of Tantra and the Tao. When you make love you are sharing the most intimate contact with one another, and the best education either of you can have is to love each other completely. You should also try to become aware of the many different forces, cycles of nature, and subtle energies that permeate every level of our very existence. Think of this education as a mutual rediscovery, one that brings an awakening to understanding each other on a physical level.

FEMALE SEXUAL ANATOMY
The mound of Venus (mons veneris), *a layer of fat covering the pubic bone, divides into the outer vaginal lips* (labia majora). *Inside these are the inner lips* (labia minora), *the urethral opening, and the entrance to the vagina. The inner lips join at the top to form the "hood" that protects the highly sensitive head of the clitoris when it is in its unerect state; pull the hood back and you will expose the clitoris.*

FEMALE SEXUAL ANATOMY

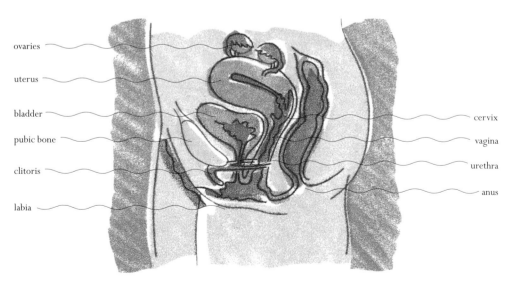

ovaries
uterus
bladder
pubic bone
clitoris
labia

cervix
vagina
urethra
anus

THE G-SPOT

During sexual excitement, a concentration of blood vessels surrounding the urethra, and known as the urethral sponge, swells with blood. This creates a bulge that can be felt through the vaginal wall at a point called the G-spot, named after its discoverer, the German gynecologist Ernest Gräfenberg. It is thought to be more sensitive in some women than in others.

It can be located by using a finger to explore and feel around the front and upper part of the inside of your vagina. When the spot is stimulated, either manually or by your partner's penis, you experience strong sensations of pleasure that are often accompanied by the feeling that you might urinate. If you get this far, do not hold back. Experience the sensation without fearing that you are about to urinate, because if you allow it to continue you will experience increased sexual arousal and ejaculation (see page 35).

The best positions for stimulating the G-spot during lovemaking are when you lie on your front or kneel for rear entry, or when you are on top of your partner. For some women, stimulation of the G-spot can trigger orgasm, while for others it is simply an arousing part of overall sexual stimulation.

bladder

G-spot

vagina

LOCATING THE G-SPOT
You can locate your G-spot by gently inserting a finger into your vagina and searching, on the abominal side of the vaginal wall, for an area where the tissue has a different texture—more bumpy with tiny folds. This is your G-spot. It is easier to locate it when you are squatting or lying down with your legs in the air than when sitting, standing, or lying flat

GETTING TO KNOW YOUR BODY

There is an exercise which, if you haven't already tried it, I urge you to do right now as you read this section. Take your clothes off, find a mirror, and use it to study the anatomy of your genital area, becoming familiar with all its different colors, textures, and shapes.

AROUSAL AND ORGASM

During sexual arousal, a woman's vaginal lips become swollen and their color deepens. The shaft of her clitoris thickens and shortens and becomes erect, her vagina lengthens and expands and excretes a lubricating fluid, her breasts swell, and her nipples become erect. If arousal continues, her clitoris enlarges further, but seems to disappear because it pulls back against the pubic bone and is covered by the swollen vaginal lips. Nipple erection similarly appears to decrease because of enlargement of the surrounding breast tissue.

During orgasm, a woman's heart rate more than doubles, her breathing is over three times as fast as normal, and the outer third of her vagina (the orgasmic platform) contracts rhythmically, typically from three to 15 times in as many seconds.

FEMALE EROGENOUS ZONES

FRONT AND SIDES

The principle erogenous zones on a woman's front and sides are the insides of her arms, her breasts and nipples, and her waist, genital region, and thighs. On her head, her scalp, ears, cheeks, lips, eyelids, throat, and neck will all respond erotically to delicate touch and kisses.

In conventional terms, an erogenous zone is any part of the body that triggers sexual arousal when it is stimulated. In Tantric and Taoist tradition and in many ancient love texts, however, the entire body is an erogenous zone that can be awakened by the mind. Once awakened, the body responds through the sense organs, activating subtle channels and freeing energy to circulate. In the Hindu love manual the *Ananga Ranga*, for example, the erogenous zones of a woman's body are said to be the head, eyes, lips, mouth, cheeks, ears, throat, nape of neck, breasts, nipples, belly, back, arms, hands, thighs, knees, ankles, feet, big toes, vulva, waist, buttocks, the crown of the head, and the center of the forehead, a list that includes just about every part of the body.

The ancient Tantrists and Taoists also believed that various "passions" in a woman were located in different parts of her body at different phases of the moon. In the Tantric teachings, certain rituals were prescribed for specific days in the moon's cycle, and these included stimulation of particular areas of a woman's body. This thinking is reflected in the *Ananga Ranga*, which states that passion resides in a woman's right side from the new moon to the full moon, and in her left side from full moon to new moon.

The *Ananga Ranga* also recommends ways of stimulating a woman's erogenous zones in order to arouse her. For example, it advises that her head and hair should be stimulated by holding her hair and caressing her head with the fingertips, and her lips should be sucked and softly bitten.

There are many ways to stimulate a woman's erogenous zones, such as kissing, licking, biting, nibbling, kneading, rubbing, brushing, caressing, and squeezing. Giving her a sensual massage (see page 102) is an excellent way of discovering her less obvious erogenous zones and finding how she likes to be touched in those places.

SELF-EXAMINATION

A woman can learn a lot about her own erogenous zones by examining and exploring her naked body in front of a mirror. However, self-examination is very difficult for some people, because an "inner critic" pops up and notices anything that could be considered an imperfection, so they prefer to stay clothed and keep it all covered.

But we are composed of much more than the mere physical, and loving yourself gives you self-confidence, which is always more attractive than self-deprecation. Examine your naked body, appreciate it for what it is, notice what you like about your body or face—there is always something. How does it make you feel? How do other parts of your body make you feel?

Breathe love into these areas, smile at yourself, tell yourself you are beautiful, and believe it. Once you are able to appreciate and love your body fully, you will be more inspired to honor it, which might bring about all kinds of changes in different levels of your life.

Learning to love and appreciate your physical body is only one aspect of self-examination. To be able to get the most out of the Tantric and Taoist sexual practices it is important to be able to turn your attention from your outward appearance and focus inward. Give yourself time to reflect and contemplate on your connection with everything that is, and to understand the causes behind your actions and your reactions to different situations. Try to develop an awareness of your true self, your inner self which is masked from view to others.

SELF-DISCOVERY

Working with a mirror is a very powerful tool of self-discovery. Watch how different thoughts and feelings change your facial expression, then replace any negative thoughts or attitudes with positive ones and notice the physical changes that follow.

Use your imagination to create rituals that will replace any negativity you have about yourself with a positive attitude. For example, write down on a piece of paper everything you want to let go of in your life. Then burn it to transmute the negative, harmful energy that it now represents into positive, nourishing energy. Or take a ritual bath, using the water to wash away whatever worries you, and asking it to cleanse and purify your psyche.

BACK

The line of a woman's spine, from the back of her neck down to the cleft between her buttocks, is one of her most highly sensitive erogenous zones. Her buttocks, richly endowed with nerve endings, are also very erogenous, as are the backs of her legs.

THE PC MUSCLE

In both men and women, the pelvic floor is made up of two groups of muscles. The first, the outer front muscles, include the bulbocavernosus, ischiocavernosus, and urethral sphincter muscles. The second group, the inner rear muscles near the anus, include the pubococcygeus, iliococcygeus, and levator ani muscles.

The pubococcygeus, or pubococcygeal (PC) muscle, is also known as the "love muscle" because tensing it during intercourse tightens the grip of the vagina on the penis. It stretches from the pubic bone to the coccyx, and it is the muscle that you use when you are desperate to urinate but need to hold it in. The easiest way of locating it is to try stopping and starting your flow of urine. The muscle you will then be using is your PC.

Like all muscles, the PC benefits from exercise, and keeping it toned promotes healthy sexual functioning for both men and women. During orgasm, in both men and women, the PC contracts at the rate of about once every 0.8 seconds for up to 15 seconds.

The benefits of exercising the pelvic floor muscle groups, including the PC muscle, are numerous. These exercises allow you to get in touch with your genitals and sexual feelings and make orgasm more voluntary, and help to firm and tone the vagina after childbirth. Being able to contract your PC muscle voluntarily during lovemaking will also help build up your arousal, because it improves the blood flow to the area, bringing energy and feeling to the vagina, clitoris, and G-spot.

urethra

vagina

anus

PC MUSCLE EXERCISES

Long before the 1950's, when a Los Angeles physician called Arnold Kegel developed the pelvic floor muscle exercises that bear his name, ancient experts had identified PC muscle control as a way of achieving, intensifying, prolonging, and controlling orgasm in both sexes. Contracting the PC and anal muscles was also used as a locking method to stop energy leaking out of the body.

To exercise your PC muscle, begin by tightening and relaxing it in a rhythmic, pumping action. Start by tightening and relaxing the muscle 20 times, twice a day. You can do it standing, sitting, or lying down, wherever you are and whatever else you are doing—writing, reading, working, waiting for a bus, train, or plane—and the joy is that it is pleasurable. Extremely pleasurable! Gradually build up the number of contractions, but take care not to overdo it and make the muscle sore. You might find that, at first, tensing your PC muscle also tenses other muscles, such as those of your abdomen, but you will soon be able to isolate the contractions so that the rest of your body stays relaxed.

Once you are familiar with the pumping action, extend your exercise routine by tightening your PC muscle, holding it tight for as long as you can, and then completely relaxing. Again start with about 20 at a time and gradually build up the number, but be sure to relax the muscle completely between each contraction. Focus your attention on the sensations that are created in your genitals and don't be surprised if they feel erotic—enjoy them.

Combining breath control (see page 54) with the tensing and relaxing of your PC muscle will greatly enhance the sensations. Inhale as you tense the muscle, keeping the rest of your body relaxed, and draw the sensation from your genitals up through your body. Then exhale, push down as if "bearing down," and let all your muscles relax completely before repeating.

It takes little more than two months of practice to strengthen and tone the PC muscle, and the results that you will experience during lovemaking will inspire you to continue with the exercises.

ENHANCED LOVEMAKING

As your control over your PC muscle increases, incorporate the tense/relax action in your lovemaking. You can lie motionless in union with your partner, and make love by contracting and relaxing your PC muscle without either of you having to use any other muscle. Being able to make love "internally" like this, without relying solely on your partner's thrusting power, brings new and great heights of pleasure for both of you. You will also experience orgasms more easily by clenching and relaxing your PC, either while self-pleasuring or during lovemaking.

Another enjoyable way to use your PC muscle control is to relax the muscle as your partner thrusts and squeeze it tight as he withdraws. Eventually, you will have enough muscle control to make your vagina grip either the whole penis or short sections of it.

USING THE PC MUSCLE
The Kama Sutra *refers indirectly to using the PC muscle in its description of the "mare's position." This is not actually a lovemaking posture, but a technique in which the woman grips the man's penis tightly in her vagina. It can be used in any posture, including that depicted here.*

ORGASM

Orgasm is a very different experience for men and women, and neither can really know what making love feels like to the other. For men, the most pleasurable part of lovemaking is usually the intense excitement of ejaculation, so their sexual goal is to reach that peak and they are capable of getting there very quickly. Women, however, generally need more time and stimulation for the sexual energy to rise. In the Taoist tradition, man is fire, woman is water: his sexual energy heats up quickly then explodes, hers is like a pan of cool water that takes time to come to a boil and time to cool down again.

As well as taking longer to become sexually aroused, women experience orgasm in a multitude of ways, ranging from the subtle to the explosive. The experience varies from one woman to another, and for each individual woman according to her emotional, mental, and physical well-being plus a host of subtle underlying factors. So my advice to women is to forget about orgasm as the goal of your lovemaking and just enjoy each moment, focusing on the physical sensations.

MUTUAL SATISFACTION

Female satisfaction was of great importance for the ancient Tantrists and Taoists. The woman was considered an open channel of life-giving forces and men were taught how to arouse a woman while controlling their ejaculation, and to sustain the ecstatic peak of pleasure, which is both healing and inspirational.

Tantrists and Taoists both believe that energy rises through the body as sexual arousal and excitement increase. For the Tantrists, the sexual energy moves up through the four main chakras of the body (solar plexus, heart, throat, and brow), activating each one in turn.

Taoists view the rising energy as spreading into the body's major organs. In Dr. Stephen Chang's book, *The Tao of Sexology,* the female orgasm has been divided into nine levels, the woman's response to each level being an indication of how the sexual energy is moving through her body and energizing different parts of it.

What most women experience as orgasm is only, on this basis, level four. But the rewards for the man in being able to retain his semen (see page 46) and so bring his lover through all nine stages of orgasm are immense. The man's satisfaction is multiplied, and his pleasure is increased, as he holds back and experiences the sensations of tension and relaxation. He can then gradually bring himself to a peak, having lovingly served his partner.

Both partners are required to stimulate and retain, exchanging roles to promote the release of the maximum amount of sexual energy. The man needs to be able to retain his semen and the woman must completely surrender herself to the waves of energy and the urge to climax.

CLITORAL AND VAGINAL ORGASMS

Female orgasm has been divided into two types, the clitoral and the vaginal. A clitoral orgasm is the result of clitoral stimulation and is localized in the genital region. A vaginal orgasm is the result of vaginal and G-spot stimulation and is felt deeper in the body, as a series of waves.

However, as we are all different we are all capable of experiencing orgasm in a multitude of ways and there are no hard and fast rules. Aim to educate yourself about your sexual anatomy, to release unnatural feelings of guilt and shame, and to open yourself to your sexuality so as to experience the maximum pleasure.

FEMALE EJACULATION

Ejaculation is not limited to men alone—some women are also capable of it when highly aroused! During sexual arousal, the initial lubricative fluid is produced from the wall of the vagina and is known as the "first water"; the "second water" is emitted during orgasm.

The "third water" is an ejaculatory fluid possibly released from glands within the urethral sponge (see page 29). Most women never experience this release because the sensation makes them feel that they are urinating and so they hold back. The ejaculation can produce varying amounts of clear, almost watery fluid.

THE NINE LEVELS OF FEMALE ORGASM

According to The Tao of Sexology, *the nine levels of female orgasm are:*

LEVEL	ENERGIZED ORGANS	WOMAN'S RESPONSE
One	Lungs	*She sighs and breathes heavily and salivates*
Two	Heart	*She extends her tongue while kissing the man*
Three	Spleen, pancreas, and stomach	*Her muscles become activated, and she grasps and holds him tightly*
Four	Kidneys and bladder	*Vaginal spasms start and fluids begin to flow*
Five	Bones	*Her joints loosen and she bites the man*
Six	Liver and nerves	*She undulates and gyrates, wrapping her arms and legs around him*
Seven	Blood	*Her blood is "boiling" and she tries to touch him everywhere*
Eight	Muscles	*Her muscles relax, she bites and grabs his nipples*
Nine	Whole body	*She completely surrenders to the man and opens up*

Menstruation

The monthly cycle is a different experience for every woman, influenced by her cultural and religious beliefs as well as the myriad of symptoms that precede, accompany, and follow menstruation.

For the Taoists, conservation of energy was of prime importance, and they viewed menstruation as a loss of valuable energy. Their solution to this was what is known as the Deer Exercise for Women, which is said to reverse the energy loss by minimizing or stopping menstruation. It consists of a series of self-massage strokes involving the breasts and vagina, and the contraction of the anal sphincter and the PC muscle (see page 32). In addition to helping control menstruation, the exercise is believed to encourage sexual energy and keep a woman youthful. A description of the Deer Exercise can be found in Dr. Stephen Chang's book *The Tao of Sexology,* and for more detailed information, I recommend Mantak and Maneewan Chia's *Cultivating Female Sexual Energy.*

THE MONTHLY CYCLE
The length of the menstrual cycle varies from one woman to another, but is usually about 28 days. Menstruation itself is essentially the shedding of the lining of the womb, which occurs every month unless the woman becomes pregnant. The hormones that are released at different stages of the cycle can have a profound effect on a woman's mood.

The corpus luteum grows for a few days and produces a hormone, progesterone, before withering away when menstruation begins at about 28 days after the beginning of the cycle

After releasing the egg, the ruptured follicle becomes a structure known as a corpus luteum

The menstrual cycle begins with the maturing of an ovarian follicle, within one of the two ovaries, from which an ovum (egg) will be released

During the first week of the cycle, the follicle grows and produces the hormone estrogen

During the second week of the cycle, the follicle continues to grow and produce estrogen, and moves to the surface of the ovary

Halfway through the menstrual cycle, at ovulation, the follicle releases the ovum, which passes into one of the fallopian tubes. If it

is then fertilized by a sperm, the ovum will implant in the lining of the womb, pregnancy will begin, and menstruation will not occur

Attitudes to Menstruation

A great deal of fear is associated with the power of menstrual blood. In ancient cultures worldwide (and today in some tribes in parts of Asia and Africa) it was customary for menstruating women to separate themselves from their normal activities. Special arrangements were made for them so they would not have to cook for others, participate in religious practices, or bathe in communal places. This was because it was recognized that a menstruating woman is more open and receptive to psychic forces.

In the West, we have developed ways of being very discreet about our periods and having little or no physical contact with this "stuff" that our bodies produce once a month. Unless we experience severe discomfort or pain, we tend to try and ignore it and get on with our daily activities. Denying menstruation, even hating it, is a fundamental part of most women's experience of it. But recognizing it as a powerful, receptive time, one of purification and renewal deserving of honor in whichever way you choose, will make a great difference to how you experience it.

And, of course, men need to be aware of its special nature and to treat their partners more protectively, allowing them the space to vary their daily routines and offering them seclusion, if that is their desire.

Menstrual Rituals

Tantric yogis view a menstruating woman as the embodiment of the Mother Kali, the goddess and initiator of transcendence: during menstruation, a woman becomes a doorway to other worlds. There are also Tantric texts that credit making love to a menstruating partner with the power of rejuvenation.

For a woman, intercourse during menstruation can greatly reduce cramps and discomfort, and the best postures to use are those in which the woman is on top of the man. These allow her to take the active role, allowing her energy and blood to flow downward. It is important to assume postures that allow this downward flow, and supine postures are not recommended during menstruation because the flow is restricted and can be pushed upward, which could be harmful for the woman.

A potent ritual to perform, either alone or with an intimate partner, is to place your finger inside your vagina and then dot your forehead with your menstrual blood. Give yourself time to meditate afterwards, or to sit quietly without distraction, or perform the ritual before you go to sleep at night. My lover and I share this ritual and, for us, the effects are quite profound. Being able to share the power of this experience with a partner who is open to view the woman with reverence and awe, understanding and respect, is a very purifying and powerful act, not to be abused.

THE MALE PARTNER

As with the section on The Female Partner (see page 28), I hope that both men and women will read the information that follows, so as to gain an insight into male sexuality and how it can be enhanced.

One of the greatest pleasures a man can experience during lovemaking is when his partner surrenders herself to him and opens like a blossoming lotus. Her feminine Yin essence or energy (see page 15), in its most potent form, is then balanced with his masculine Yang energy and their lovemaking becomes a mutually fulfilling experience, opening the gateway to greater self-awareness and promoting health and vitality.

But if a woman is always left unsatisfied by her partner, the result is an imbalance of energy that affects both partners, physically and emotionally. To ensure his partner's sexual satisfaction, a man needs to give her adequate foreplay (see page 108) and needs the capacity to control or delay his ejaculation by using semen retention techniques (see page 46). To do this, he requires an understanding of his sexual anatomy and how it works.

THE MALE GENITALS
Sperm is produced in each testicle and stored in its adjacent epididymis. From there, it travels via the vas deferens tubes and into the seminal vesicles, where seminal fluid is produced and stored until ejaculation. The seminal vesicles are connected to the prostate gland, which surrounds the urethra above the anus and in front of the bladder. Prostatic fluid secreted by the prostate gland is the major component of semen.

MALE SEXUAL ANATOMY

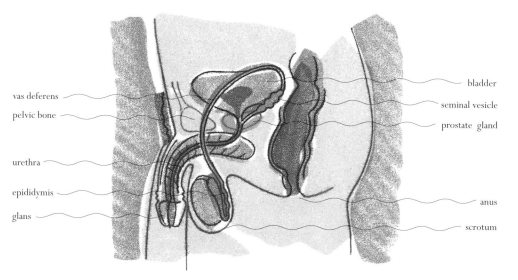

vas deferens

pelvic bone

urethra

epididymis

glans

bladder

seminal vesicle

prostate gland

anus

scrotum

THE PROSTATE GLAND

The prostate is a chestnut-shaped gland that surrounds the urethra near the point at which it leaves the bladder. It becomes enlarged during sexual arousal, and secretes a clear fluid that is an important constituent of semen. During ejaculation, the gland contracts rhythmically to help propel the semen along the urethra. The pleasurable sensations that accompany ejaculation are partly created by this contracting and relaxing of the prostate gland.

Like a woman's G-Spot (see page 29), a man's prostate gland is highly sensitive to stimulation, and most men find this extremely pleasant, particularly when they are approaching orgasm.

Use a finger to locate your prostate gland and become familiar with the size, shape, and feel of it, and discover how it enlarges during arousal. Gentle massage of the prostate is beneficial, particularly if you practice semen retention (see page 46), and can be very pleasurable, particularly if your partner does it for you.

Use gentle pressure, wash your hands before and after, and make sure your fingernails are short.

penis

prostate gland

testicles

LOCATING THE PROSTATE GLAND
You should be able to feel your prostate through the front wall of your anus by gently inserting a finger and pressing up and toward your navel. Sometimes it is also possible to stimulate your prostate externally by applying pressure to your perineum, the area of skin between your scrotum and your anus. Regular prostate examination and massage will alert you to any potentially unhealthy changes in its condition.

GETTING TO KNOW YOUR BODY

The principal parts of a man's genitalia are his penis, testicles (testes), and his prostate gland (see above). The penis is made up of spongelike tissues surrounding the urethra, a thin tube that runs through its center and along which urine and semen are discharged. The two testicles are enclosed within a bag of skin called the scrotum. Each is suspended by a spermatic cord that supplies it with blood and nerve connections, and provides a duct (the vas deferens) along which sperm passes after it has been produced by the testicle.

When a man becomes sexually aroused, the spongelike tissues of his penis become engorged with blood, making it swell, stiffen, and become erect. As he nears ejaculation (see page 44), his testicles are drawn up toward his body, the wall of his scrotum thickens and tightens, and his blood pressure, heart rate, breathing rate, and skin temperature increase.

Rhythmic contractions of the prostate, seminal vesicles, and vas deferens pump semen into the base of the urethra. When ejaculation occurs, the semen is forced along the urethra and out of the tip of the penis by another series of contractions, this time of the urethra and the muscles of the base and shaft of the penis.

MALE EROGENOUS ZONES

Erogenous zones are areas of the body that are particularly sensitive to stimulation. Although these vary from individual to individual, the main erogenous zones of a man tend to be the penis, navel, chest, nipples, thighs, hands, feet, tongue, ears, and neck; less obvious areas are the armpits, eyelids, scrotum, and prostate. But the most prominent erogenous zone—for women as well as men—is the mind. Stir the imagination and the body responds through its sense organs.

FRONT AND SIDES
The principle erogenous zones on a man's front and sides are his neck, ears, and throat, his armpits, his chest and nipples, the area between his navel and his genitals, the genitals themselves, his perineum, and the insides of his thighs. Stroking or kissing his hands and feet is also likely to arouse him.

PATTERNS OF AROUSAL
Male sexual energy is quite different to female sexual energy. The vast majority of women take much longer to be aroused than do most men. The sexual heat in a man rises quickly and explodes, while a woman takes time to be brought to the boil, but when a man can control his excitement and help his partner to reach the heights of sexual arousal, the rewards for both are extraordinary. It is well worth taking time to learn your own reactions to touch, and how to control them while you are stimulating your partner, so that you can match your level of arousal to hers. This will also help you to control your ejaculation, and make it much easier for you to practice semen retention (see page 46), which will benefit both you and your partner.

NEW EXPERIENCES
Turn your senses inward and experience your body from the inside as you stimulate it in different ways on the outside. Give your masculine, logical, thinking mind a rest and let your feminine, intuitive, imaginative side take over. This will not only help you to enjoy the stimulation you are giving yourself, but will often also make you aware of any inhibitions you have about your body. If you have any such inhibitions, identifying and acknowledging them will help you to come to terms with them and, with a little effort, you should eventually be able to overcome them. Learning about yourself in this way will help you to experience lovemaking with your mind and your whole body, instead of with just your genitals.

Self-pleasuring

Most of us, from a very young age, are taught that self-pleasuring is something to be ashamed of. It therefore becomes something that we practice in secret, and finish as quickly as possible to reduce the risk of being discovered. So for a lot of men, self-pleasuring becomes a form of quick release, usually limited to stimulating the penis.

This unnecessary limit to self-pleasuring can have a number of negative consequences. It can create a sense of guilt about your sexuality, and it denies you the enjoyment to be gained from unhurried self-pleasuring. It also teaches you very little about your responses to different sorts of touch and stimulation, and knowledge of these is something that you, and your partner, can put to good use during your lovemaking.

Here is an exercise in self-pleasuring which I urge you to try, if you haven't already. Take a leisurely, luxurious bath and cleanse yourself as if preparing to make love. Then become your ideal lover and make love to yourself, using your thoughts, imagination, and the physical sensations of touching and caressing yourself. Leave no part of you unexplored—don't limit your touching to your genitals—and give yourself the greatest amount of pleasure you can manage.

Notice how the different parts of your body respond to touch, and how these responses make you feel. Try to stimulate yourself to an increasingly higher level of sexual arousal while avoiding the temptation to ejaculate too quickly: bring yourself slowly to boiling point.

For this exercise avoid external stimulation such as magazines or videos; simply embark on a voyage of self-discovery, free of fear, guilt, and shame, making love to yourself and getting in touch with your own emotional and physical responses. Self-pleasuring is an important physical aspect of self-examination, which is also about going inside yourself and discovering your true inner nature through meditation and contemplation, searching out and freeing any blockages so that energy can flow through your physical and your subtle body.

BACK

The erogenous zones of a man's back include the back of his neck, the line of his spine, his buttocks and the cleft between them, the backs of his thighs, and the hollows at the backs of his knees.

PENIS SIZE AND SHAPE

Because male and female genitals are as diverse in shape, size, and appearance as their owners, there is no overall "perfect" size for a penis. The Taoist viewpoint is that the ideal penis is one that fits the vagina perfectly. Some women have long vaginas, which more easily accommodate a long penis, and others have short vaginas more suitable for shorter penises. The vagina is capable of expanding to take a generous width, but care should be taken on penetration, and attempting entry before a woman is ready can be harmful to her. When a woman is ready to receive you, her vulva will open like a flower, and you should arouse her so that her vaginal secretions become a natural lubricant.

TRADITIONAL BELIEFS

In the classic Hindu love manuals—the *Kama Sutra* and the *Ananga Ranga*—men and women are categorized by the size, shape, and secretions of their genitals. These characteristics are said to be accompanied by various other distinctive physical attributes, such as the sound of the voice, the shape of the hips or waist, and the movement of the body.

In Taoist sexology, the shape and size of a woman's lips are considered a clear indication of the shape and size of her vagina. Similarly, the thickness of a man's lips is said to reflect the thickness of his penis, while the shape of his thumb indicates its shape and proportions.

Just as women need to let go of insecurities about their physical appearance, so do most men, particularly in relation to the size of their penises. I believe that if men can let go of their obsessions with penis size, or lack of it, women will stop teasing them about it!

PENIS EXERCISES

In general, a man has to face the fact that, unless he resorts to expensive surgery, he must accept his penis as the size and shape it is and realize that, in its own way, it is perfect. But although the size and shape of a man's penis is determined at birth, it is sometimes possible for him to make minor improvements to it by practicing certain simple exercises.

If your penis is "pencil-shaped," with a wide shaft but a smaller, pointed glans (head), you can encourage the glans to increase in size. To do this, squeeze your penis along its length as if milking it, forcing the blood to flow into the glans. It takes practice, but over a period of time you should notice the head becoming bigger and more mushroom-like in shape. This shape is considered more satisfying for a woman because a large head provides a thorough massage and stimulation of the walls of the vagina and the G-spot.

To help strengthen your erection and genital muscle control, try "weightlifting" with your penis. Hang a small washcloth over your erect penis, contract your muscles, and see how far you can raise it. As your strength improves, increase the weight from a washcloth to a small towel and eventually to a bath towel—a wet one!

Another exercise is simply to squeeze the shaft of your penis until it becomes rock hard. Repeated squeezing stimulates the blood flow in the spongelike tissues of the penis (see page 39), and should help to produce increasingly firm erections.

You can improve your overall genital fitness by exercising your pubococcygeal (PC) muscle (see below), and by toning up the other muscles in your pelvic area. To do this, tense the muscles in your thighs, buttocks, and abdomen, hold them taut for as long as you can, and then relax. Repeat this as often as you can; eventually you should be able to continue the exercise for about five minutes at a time.

PC Muscle Exercises

When you have learned how to control your pubococcygeal (PC) muscle, you will be able to separate orgasmic response from ejaculation. This will enable you to preserve your precious Yang essence while still experiencing the pleasures of orgasm, allowing both you and your partner to discover new levels of sexual ecstasy.

The PC, like any other muscle in the body, can be toned, strengthened, and developed by regular exercise. The exercises are simple—they can be performed any time, any place, anywhere—and involve isolating the muscle and repeatedly contracting and releasing it in a pumping action. Start with a routine of about 20 contractions once a day, finding your own rhythm, and gradually build up so that you can comfortably do about 75 contractions twice a day. As you

penis

anus

become more adept at controlling and exercising your PC, incorporate breath control into your routine. Inhale, contract your PC, and hold it tight while you retain the breath, and then relax the muscle completely when you exhale.

Having control of your PC muscle will also help you to practice semen retention (see page 46). Soon after you begin to exercise regularly, you will notice that by contracting your PC when you are on the threshold of orgasm, you can delay ejaculation. With practice and a little effort, you will eventually manage to experience orgasm without ejaculation.

Contracting the PC muscle also massages and stimulates the prostate gland. This prevents stagnation and congestion in the prostate, and is essential if you practice semen retention.

MALE ORGASM

For a man, orgasm is the third of the four main stages of his sexual response cycle. It is preceded by desire and arousal (see page 39), and followed by a period of variable length called the refractory phase. During the refractory phase, the physical changes that occurred during arousal and orgasm are slowly reversed and his body returns to normal. Some men may be able to achieve another erection during the refractory phase, but usually not an ejaculation.

ORGASM AND EJACULATION
Although orgasm and ejaculation are conventionally thought of as being identical, Tantrists and Taoists regard them as separate and believe that it is possible for men, like most women, to experience orgasm without ejaculation.

For men, the peak sensations of ejaculation—which they tend to associate with orgasm—last only a few seconds. These are essentially genital sensations and are normally followed by mental and physical exhaustion as the body begins the process of replacing lost fluids.

When ejaculation occurs (see page 39), the muscle that closes off the exit from the bladder clamps shut. This prevents the semen entering the bladder and ensures that it is pumped along the urethra and out of the tip of the penis. It is estimated that the average man will ejaculate about 5,000 times in his lifetime, and each ejaculation contains up to a teaspoon (5 ml) of semen.

That teaspoonful of semen consists of up to 500 million sperm plus a valuable mixture of nutrients such as proteins and sugars. The Taoists believe that it also contains life energy, and that by limiting the number of times he ejaculates, a man can thus conserve his life energy and live a happier, livelier, and longer life.

ENDLESS LOVEMAKING
Using semen retention to permit orgasm without ejaculation has been practiced for thousands of years and is very much a part of the Tantric and Taoist traditions. It is not something to fear and, if mastered, the benefits that accrue—physical, psychological, spiritual, and emotional—are a worthy reward for both partners.

Both Taoists and Tantric yogis were involved in the development of physical and mental methods of controlling and regulating ejaculation (see page 46) in order to cultivate sexual energy and generate states of blissful ecstasy.

For ejaculation control to be successful, it is necessary for women to understand its psychological aspects. Part of my sexual education, or rather my lack of it, was being taught that the goal of intercourse was orgasm, and that male orgasm was ejaculation. His semen was proof that he loved me, and confirmation that I was a good lover. If he didn't ejaculate, I felt as though I had failed, and that I wasn't exciting enough as a lover.

My understanding of it now—having experienced the effects with my partner, who willingly retains his semen—is that our lovemaking has no end. The goal is no longer to get excited as quickly as possible then lose ourselves in a rush of explosive release, but to cultivate and increase sexual energy and move it through our bodies. The eventual release through ejaculation out of the body then becomes a rush of energy that moves inside the body. This is accompanied by what feels like an almost unlimited experience of orgasm, during which an exchange of energies takes place—he receives my Yin essence to balance his Yang energy, and I receive Yang energy from him. Every cell of our beings vibrates with sexual ecstasy.

SEMEN RETENTION

Semen retention, or ejaculation control, is not simply the stopping of ejaculation, although that is its most important aspect. It is about a man transforming his ching or sexual energy (see page 17) and circulating it in his body so that he becomes physically and spiritually nourished. When he has become sensitive to the energy flows within his body, he can draw it up his spine from his genital region and push it down the front of his body in order to circulate the energy between him and his partner during lovemaking. This creates an energy circuit where the negative and positive forces, Yin and Yang, are exchanged and individuals become one in perfect balance and harmony.

Another benefit of semen retention is that when a man retains and reabsorbs his sexual fluids into his system, it maintains and intensifies his sexual identity. When this happens, he will invariably experience a greater, longer-lasting attraction for his partner and an enhanced intimacy with her. This will bring a heightened intensity of pleasure, a regeneration of physical health, and a contribution to spiritual growth. But the only way you are going to know its effects is to try it.

How each man should regulate his ejaculation depends on his age, state of health, and lifestyle. As a guideline, take your age, multiply it by 2, then divide it by 10. For example, if you are thirty years old, 30 years multiplied by 2 divided by 10 = 6. This is the minimum number of days that you should allow between each ejaculation in order to preserve your life force without restricting your lovemaking.

But by becoming more sensitive to your own energy and to your personal needs, you will establish your own rhythm. In controlling ejaculation and encouraging the flow of energy, you will find that your body becomes strengthened and more alive to sensation. And allowing lovemaking to continue for longer gives greater fulfilment to the woman—satisfying a woman's sexual needs is an important aspect of the Tao of loving.

SEMEN RETENTION TECHNIQUES

There are a number of different practices and techniques that a man can use to help him control his ejaculation, retain his semen, and cultivate his sexual energy. These can help you to prolong lovemaking by delaying your ejaculation, and when you are adept at them you will be able to have orgasms—felt as a long series of slow, pleasurable spasms and a flow of energy—without ejaculating.

These basic semen retention techniques can be used singly or in combination, depending on your individual needs and abilities. But if you have a problem with your prostate gland, please consult your physician before attempting any semen retention exercises.

BREATHING AND THRUSTING

One of the physiological effects associated with ejaculation is a rapid increase in heart rate (see page 39), and if you can keep your heart rate close to normal during intercourse you will be able to delay your urge to ejaculate.

A good way to regulate your heart rate while you are making love is to take deep, rhythmic breaths, which will help you to avoid getting carried away with excitement. Breath control (see page 54) is even more effective as a semen retention technique when you combine it with frequent use of the *Mula bandha,* or "root lock," the breathing technique that involves contraction of the anal sphincter (see page 55).

You can make your breath control even more effective by combining it with control of your thrusting. Another aspect of male ejaculation is that the speed and depth of your thrusting increase as ejaculation approaches. When you feel that ejaculation is approaching, make your thrusts shallow and slow. This type of thrusting has the added benefit of enabling you to move in such a way that it is the relatively insensitive upper surface of your penis that is receiving the most friction. The way to do this is to keep it in contact with your partner's highly sensitive clitoris, thus greatly increasing her stimulation while reducing your own.

If shallow thrusting proves inadequate to stave off the ejaculatory urge, try partially or totally withdrawing from your partner until you have calmed down a little. Continue to stimulate her manually until you feel ready to resume intercourse.

PRESSURE TECHNIQUE

A traditional Taoist method of ejaculation control is simultaneous contraction of the PC muscle (see page 43) and the anal sphincter. If you cannot do this successfully, try pressing the index and middle fingers of one hand against a point on your perineum halfway between your anus and your scrotum (learn where this point is before using the technique). This will prevent semen from leaving your prostate and entering your urethra for ejaculation.

III

....

YOGA

YOGA

The word "yoga" is a Sanskrit word meaning "joining" or "yoking," signifying the union of the individual self with pure consciousness, or God. Hatha Yoga, the yoga of the physical body, is a discipline that includes thousands of different asanas (postures). These were inspired by nature and designed to keep mind and body in perfect health with energies flowing freely and effectively.

Most of the people to whom I teach yoga are surprised by what they are able to achieve in a comparatively short time, and the difference they feel in their bodies is immediate. This is because, on the whole, most of us live very sedentary lives and get very little exercise, and we take our bodies and their internal functioning for granted. As long as everything is working well, we make no attempt to improve it, so as soon as we begin any form of regular exercise, including yoga, the beneficial effects soon become apparent.

Generally, we are not good about taking time to treat our minds and bodies with respect. But however low your energy levels are at the end (or the start) of a working day, you can still practice yoga techniques, such as breath control and simple exercises, that will help you to improve your overall health and fitness.

EXERCISE

For our bodies and minds to operate at their best and be free of stress and tension, we need to exercise them. Any kind of conscious physical exercise will give you a greater awareness of your body and what it needs to be able to serve you at its fullest potential. By exercising regularly you are taking responsibility for yourself, and the good news is that it is never too late to start! Learning yoga, including re-learning how to breathe, is an excellent way to do this.

THE BENEFITS OF YOGA

Yoga is a system that not only stretches the muscles and works on the skeletal framework but also massages and tones the internal organs. The aim is to fine-tune your senses and your entire body as a whole, to be able to separate thought from feeling. Closing your eyes while practicing

> **"When mind is absorbed in itself, it is called liberation."**
>
> SWAMI SVATMARAMA

some of the yoga exercises allows you to focus your consciousness and your flow of energy inward so that you "feel" your body from the inside. When you can do that with confidence, you will be able to direct the energy of your breath to anywhere in your body, and feel the immediate difference that it makes to your physical and mental well-being. Where the mind goes, energy flows.

YOGA PRACTICE

Some people feel, as I once did, that the discipline involved in preparing the body and mind for new heights of sexual ecstasy is impossible to maintain, and the easiest thing to do is to find reasons to avoid it. Don't think of it as discipline, think of it as time you give yourself to improve the quality of your life, because you are worth it and deserve it. When this improves, it naturally follows that, for you, everything else about life improves.

If you are a complete beginner at yoga, I strongly recommend that you attend at least a few well-run classes to make sure that you know how to adopt yoga postures correctly. Then you can practice at home, instructed by books or video tapes, either as well as or instead of your yoga classes.

Begin by setting yourself the goal of practicing one posture for three minutes every day—that is the average length of a television commercial break. You will notice the difference immediately, and that may well inspire you to spend more time on your daily yoga practice.

But even if you do nothing more than exercise your eyes by reading this chapter, I hope that it will give you a greater awareness of your own body, your bodily posture, and your breathing. For instance, notice what posture and breathing pattern you are using at the moment. Now straighten your spine, breath in deeply through your nose, breath it all out, and notice how much better you feel. These simple physical actions, which are very basic yoga practices, are valuable tools that can instantly make a positive difference to your sense of well-being.

YOGA AND SEX

Yoga postures are very good preparation for various lovemaking positions, particularly the more advanced ones (see page 132). And when you are making love with a conscious intention of healing, or as an integral part of a ritual or ceremony, your body needs stamina and suppleness and your mind needs to be clear and focused. Your full mental, emotional, and physical participation is required if your lovemaking is to take you into the realms of ecstasy. So using yoga and breathing exercises to improve your physical and mental condition, and to develop an ability to focus your attention inward, is the ideal preparation for practicing Tantric lovemaking or the Taoist healing postures (see page 140).

FOOD AND DIET

It is said, with good reason, that we are what we eat. Our bodies are built from proteins, minerals, and other nutrients in our food, which also supplies the energy that fuels them. The quality of the food we ingest thus has a direct bearing on our physical and mental well-being and, according to yogic tradition, on the quality and quantity of our energy. It naturally follows that sexual energy is inextricably linked with diet.

Most of us live in a toxic world, in which our water is recycled, the air we breathe is polluted, and many of our foodstuffs have chemical additives or contain residues of pesticides, herbicides, and fertilizers. But we need food and water to survive, so unless you live on a mountain top, drinking fresh spring water, eating organically grown foods, and hunting for fresh, uncontaminated meat or fish, you need to choose your food carefully if you want to become and remain truly healthy.

Changing your diet in accordance with yogic principles can bring a great improvement in the quality of your life, but always be conscious of where your food comes from and how it affects you physically, mentally, and emotionally.

ENERGY AND HARMONY

Each of us is biochemically different and naturally affected by his or her environment and lifestyle, so it is impossible to make hard and fast rules about diet, as each person has individual needs and goals. However, you can help yourself by eating fresh, natural, wholesome foods and liquids that nourish your body and mind, and by having an awareness of how and where they were produced. In a way, by eating for good health you are reversing the gourmet philosophy of "living to eat rather than eating to live," but even if health is the main aim, that does not mean that your diet should be boring. A proper balance in your diet is the key, and will bring harmony and vitality to your life.

In Oriental medicine and yogic texts, food and diet are as important as external and internal exercise. Just as we categorize foods by their different tastes—sweet, sour, bitter, salty—the ancient Chinese categorized foods as Yin or Yang. And according to the yogic texts, food, like any matter, has vibrational qualities; these reflect the quality of the energy into which food is transformed when eaten. There are said to be three qualities or types of energy, and thus of foods, and these are known as the three *Gunas*.

THE THREE GUNAS

The Gunas—*Sattva, Rajas, and Tamas*—are the three qualities of energy in the unmanifested universe and, like Yin and Yang in the Taoist tradition, they exist together in balance and harmony. Sattva represents purity, Rajas passion, and Tamas inertia.

When energy manifests—takes form—one of the three Gunas becomes dominant over the others. In every person, one of the Gunas dominates and its nature is clearly reflected in his or her thoughts, actions, and feelings.

Try to develop an awareness of the vibrational quality of the food you eat and the liquids you drink. Then you will be able to sense its effects on you physically and emotionally and to judge what you need.

Remember—balance is the key: not just a proper balance of nutrients, but also the balance of the Gunas, and of Yin and Yang vibrating in harmony. When you achieve this balance and harmony, your physical and spiritual bodies will be able to function at their best.

SATTVIC FOODS
The Sattvic diet includes cereals, fresh fruit and vegetables, milk, butter, cheese, nuts, seeds, and honey. It is considered the purest diet for any serious yogi.

PREPARING YOUR FOOD

The energy quality of the food we eat is important but so, too, is the spirit in which the food is prepared and the energy with which it is eaten. (A perfect example of this is depicted in a wonderful film called *Like Water for Chocolate,* where the emotions of a girl preparing food were transported into the food, and all who ate it experienced what she felt.)

Because so much of our food is convenience food, neatly packaged in oven-ready disposable dishes, we actually have very little physical contact with much of the food that we eat. All too often, eating is a kind of instant gratification, a clear reflection of a "fast lifestyle." The attitude of many people seems to be, "Yes, but we just don't have the time to notice the texture and color, where it came from, or how it was grown." This is a mistake: honor your food as "life giving life for life," and as you prepare it, consciously imbue it with a positive creative energy. Singing while you cook works wonderfully!

RAJASIC FOODS
The Rajasic foods include root vegetables, hot, spicy foods, fish, salt, and stimulants such as tea and coffee.

EATING

Saying grace or blessing food before it is eaten is a common practice in many traditions and cultures. It is an opportunity to offer thanks. Before I eat, I take a moment to close my eyes, inhale deeply, and say, either silently or out loud, "'I eat in clarity" or "I eat in love," naming whatever energy I want to charge the food with. This simple gesture makes eating a conscious action and I can enjoy the food with all my senses.

Eating when you are emotionally upset or in uncongenial surroundings will have an ill effect on your body. Try to calm your mind and rid it of unpleasant or negative feelings before eating, and enjoy your meal in as peaceful an environment as possible. Be aware of the quality of your food, where it has come from, and the blessings you charge it with. Your body, mind, and spirit will appreciate you honoring the food, and you will enjoy it more.

BREATHING

Breath is life. We cannot exist without it, and the average human being inhales approximately 20,000 breaths during a 24-hour period. It is essential to our physical health and spiritual well-being. It is also a very powerful transformational tool capable of releasing toxins, purifying the body, and altering consciousness.

As you read this, become aware of how you are breathing. Notice whether your breaths are shallow or deep and where you feel them in your chest. Are you breathing through your nose or mouth? Does your breathing pattern reflect your emotional state?

Most of us breathe inadequately. We take shallow, irregular breaths through our mouths, using only the tops of our lungs.

This means we take in only a small amount of oxygen, which reduces our physical energy levels and also allows toxins to build up within the body, resulting in a lowered resistance to disease.

The average pair of lungs is capable of breathing in over six pints (about three liters) of air, but the majority of people use less than a third of their total lung capacity when breathing normally.

BREATHING TECHNIQUES

By taking full, deep breaths we oxygenate the blood and absorb more life energy, or prana, from the atmosphere (see page 16). So important is breathing to a number of Eastern philosophies that there is a branch of yoga—Pranayama—that is concerned solely with breath control and breathing exercises. Breath control is vital to the successful mastery of Tantric and Taoist love techniques, and the importance and power of correct breathing during lovemaking cannot be stressed enough.

There are numerous yogic breathing techniques and each one causes the mind and body to react in different ways.

Breathing can be used to affect the mind through the control of prana (see page 16), and correct breathing performed during yoga exercises is vital for concentration during meditation and for the channeling of energy in the body.

Proper breathing begins with proper posture. Whether you are sitting, standing, or lying down, check that your spine is straight, your shoulders relaxed, and your neck and head are in a straight line. Practice breathing in and out through the nose; it allows the maximum amount of prana to be taken in, and the air is warmed and filtered before reaching the lungs.

COMPLETE BREATH

The most basic breathing technique is called "complete breath" or "healing breath." At first, you may find that it feels very unfamiliar, but what it is attempting to do is to remind your body how it naturally breathed as a baby.

In this technique, the breath is divided into three parts: inhalation, retention, and exhalation in the ratio of 1:4:2. You breathe in for a count of one, you hold for a count of four, and then you exhale for a count of two. The simplest way to experience the sensation of a complete breath is to lie on your back on the floor, with your body comfortable and relaxed. Place the palm of your left hand over your heart and the palm of your right hand over your navel. Close your mouth and eyes.

Begin by exhaling any stale air you have in your body: push it out through your nose. Then, as you inhale, visualize sending the breath from your nose deep into your belly and allow your belly to swell with air. As your belly expands, your diaphragm will move down and massage your abdominal organs. When you exhale, concentrate on contracting your belly first and then emptying your lungs. During the contraction of your belly, your diaphragm moves up and massages your heart.

BANDHAS

The *bandhas,* powerful tools that control prana generated within the body by breathing exercises, are yoga postures that involve muscular contractions or "locks" and are practiced in conjunction with breathing. There are three basic bandhas and, once you are familiar with the breathing exercises and well practiced in them, you can start to incorporate them into your routine.

The *Mula bandha* prevents apana (one of the vital airs) escaping from the lower body. It also stimulates the base chakra, and is an aid in semen retention (see page 46). Practice the mula bandha by tightening your anal sphincter muscle and then your abdominal muscles while retaining the breath after inhalation.

The *Jalandhara bandha* is a posture that restricts the respiratory tract, preventing prana escaping from the upper body. Practice it by pressing your chin firmly against the triangular hollow behind your collarbone while holding your breath. Hold the posture for as long as you can then, when you exhale, release the bandha and lift your head.

The third of the three basic bandhas is the *Uddiyana bandha*, a posture that gives support to the lungs and balances various elements in the body. To practice it, first exhale completely and then pull your abdomen up and back toward your spine. Hold the posture, and the exhalation, for as long as possible, and then slowly inhale by relaxing your abdominal muscles.

ALTERNATE NOSTRIL BREATHING

This helps to balance the left and right sides of the brain, the central nervous system, and the pathways of the subtle body. There are six steps to one round of this exercise, and the breathing is divided into three parts: inhalation, retention, and exhalation. The ratio between these is 1:4:2—breathe in for a count of one, hold for a count of four, and then exhale for a count of two. Begin by doing three rounds and gradually build up until you can do 20 rounds or more quite comfortably. It is a wonderful way to begin your day or to use at any time you require extra energy. It is particularly beneficial before engaging in yoga.

1 Begin by sitting on the edge of a chair or cross-legged on the floor, with your spine straight, shoulders relaxed, and neck and head in a straight line. Close your eyes, or, without straining them, try to focus them on the tip of your nose. Then place the middle and index fingers of your right hand between your eyebrows.*

2 Close your left nostril with your third and fourth fingers; breathe in through your right nostril. Close that nostril with your thumb and hold the breath.

3 Breathe out through your left nostril, keeping your right nostril closed, then inhale through your left nostril. Finally, close both nostrils and hold the breath.

BREATH OF FIRE

In Pranayama, the Breath of Fire exercise is used as a means of purification. It uses rapid diaphragmatic breathing, known as pumping (not to be confused with hyperventilating), to increase the intake of oxygen so as to purify the body and rid it of any accumulated toxins. This tones the heart, stomach, and liver and clears the mind. The exercise also strengthens the solar plexus chakra (see page 18) and stimulates kundalini (see page 20). Begin by practicing 20 to 50 rounds, holding your shoulders and chest as still as possible during the exercise and keeping the breath moving low in your belly.

Exhalations should be quick, audible, and active; inhalations should be long, silent, and passive. At the end of the exercise, after focusing your energy inward, lie on your back in the Corpse Posture (see page 61). This will allow you to relax and calm your mind. Finally, while you are still lying on your back, inhale and exhale completely: take a deep breath, hold it for as long as you can, then exhale slowly.

1 Begin by taking two complete breaths (see page 55), then take another complete breath, exhaling only three-quarters of the breath. Next, contract your abdominal muscles sharply, causing a quick, audible exhalation of the last quarter of the breath through your nose.

2 Now relax the muscles as you inhale a quarter of a breath, then snap in your abdominal muscles again to exhale. Continue this inhale/exhale sequence rapidly but at your own pace, concentrating on exhalation; inhalation will happen naturally when you relax your muscles.

3 To experience your own inner universe, use your fingers to tightly shut off your senses. Close off your ears with your thumbs, and use your fingertips to close off your eyes, nostrils, and lips. Inhale, and hold your breath for as long as you can, and finally exhale, drop your hands, and relax.

MAKING THE BODY FIT

Whatever your reasons for practicing Hatha yoga—the yoga of the physical body—you will find that it works in subtle ways on many areas of your life. It is not competitive, and it does not discriminate against age, weight, or level of fitness.

Yoga postures (asanas) combined with breathing exercises (Pranayama) will help to prepare your body and mind to function more effectively on both the physical and the metaphysical levels. Asanas work by stretching and toning the muscles, exercising the spine and the entire skeletal frame, and energizing the internal organs and glands and the nervous system.

Yoga is a rejuvenating and revitalizing form of exercise. It releases both physical and mental tension and allows us to become more aware of our bodies, giving us a sense of being able to feel them from the inside.

A person's physical body is in many ways a clear reflection of his or her mental state. Life is stressful for most of us, and the stress creates tension in our bodies: our muscles tense up, which affects the way we move and, ultimately, our state of mind. Normally we pay very little attention to our bodies: we just expect them to function perfectly, like machines, and then we complain miserably when they don't. But we should remember that our bodies are not machines, but living organisms that, when cared for properly, will make life more fulfilling.

Making yoga a part of your daily routine will change your life and your relationship with your physical, mental, and subtle bodies. On the following pages you will find many beneficial yoga postures and some adapted variations of different exercises. Begin with one or two that you feel confident with, and practice them daily. You may find some of the postures more difficult than others, but with practice they will become easier.

I prefer to practice yoga naked; life energies circulate more freely and you can feel your breath on your skin. It also enables you to appreciate the beauty of your body. For me, my yoga practice is my time to make love with myself.

MEDITATION
Yoga, combined with meditation, is a wonderful way to achieve physical fitness and relieve stress.

TIPS FOR PRACTICING YOGA

Yoga postures are at their most efficacious when done first thing in the morning or early in the evening. If you are a beginner, however, I recommend that you do your yoga exercises in the morning.

Start your day by practicing one easy posture, along with some breathing exercises (see page 55), for about three minutes. It will make such a difference to the quality of your day that it will encourage you to give yourself more time to practice more postures, so that eventually yoga becomes part of your daily ritual. Just three minutes a day is all it takes to begin making these changes in your life.

Yoga is best done on an empty stomach, which is another good reason for choosing the morning for your exercises. But if you want to practice at other times, do not eat for at least two hours beforehand.

BREATHING

When practicing your yoga, don't fight with yourself; let your body and whole being surrender and relax into the posture. Your breath will do the work and your body will follow it. Unless otherwise stated, all the breathing in the following postures is in and out through the nose, keeping the tip of your tongue on the roof of your mouth. Just as there are three stages to breathing (inhalation, retention, and exhalation) there are three stages to every posture—getting into it, staying in it, and coming out of it. All three stages must be performed correctly if you are to get the posture right, particularly if you don't have a teacher and you are performing the exercises on your own.

YOGA FOR TWO

It can be a very exciting and educational experience to practice different yoga postures with your partner, especially when you are both completely naked. It gives you a wonderful opportunity to examine your body and that of your partner in different postures, and to feel your breath on your skin, and to have close skin-on-skin contact.

After your practice, lie next to each other with one hand on your heart center and the other cupped over your partner's genitals. Breathe together as you feel your energies merge.

PRECAUTIONS

If you are suffering from any medical condition—especially one that affects your heart, nervous system, spine, neck, or bones—or if you are pregnant, have recently been injured, or undergone surgery, take advice from your doctor or a qualified yoga teacher before attempting any exercises. Because some of the postures cause internal movement, women with IUDs are advised to have regular check-ups to make sure that their devices have not moved. Menstruating women should avoid any of the inverted postures.

THE GODDESS POSTURE

In this posture, you can visualize directing the energy of your breath through your genitals. Breathe in and out through your nose, and as you inhale, feel it move up your spine to the crown of your head. Hold it there, and then exhale and feel the energy moving down the front of your body and out through your genitals. Take long breaths. To come out of this posture, very slowly bring your knees together, stopping for a moment at the point where your inner thighs begin to vibrate before closing your knees together. Then stretch your legs out on the floor.

*L*ie on your back with your feet together and heels close to your body. Stretch your arms out, palms up, then relax and let your knees fall to either side.

THE SURRENDER POSTURE

In this version of the Goddess Posture, you bring your knees together as you inhale and let them fall to either side again when you exhale. To come out of the posture, bring your knees together very slowly, and hold them for as long as possible at the point where they begin to tremble. Then slide your legs flat on the floor.

2 Let your knees fall slowly to the sides again, while exhaling through your mouth. While doing this exercise, try clenching your PC muscle (see pages 32 and 43) as you inhale and relaxing it as you exhale.

1 Lie down on your back with your knees bent, feet together, and heels close to your body. Tuck your chin in. Let your knees fall to either side, then slowly bring them together while inhaling a deep breath through your mouth.

THE BUTTERFLY POSTURE

This helps to increase flexibility in the ankles, knees, and hips. It is important to keep your spine straight, and if you find this difficult, try putting a corner of a cushion behind you under your buttocks. This posture is also a good warm-up position for sitting postures like the Lotus and for breathing exercises.

Sit on the floor with your spine straight, shoulders relaxed, knees bent, and the soles of your feet touching. Hold your feet with your hands and gently move your knees up and down like butterfly wings.

THE CORPSE POSTURE

This whole-body relaxation posture looks simple, but it is important to get in and out of it carefully. Practice it between other postures to rest your body, and when you come out of it, roll onto your left and use your arms to walk yourself gently up to a sitting position.

1 Lie on your back with your legs slightly apart, your arms falling away from your body, and your palms upward.

2 From the pelvis, rotate your legs in and out, and then let them fall gently out to the sides.

3 Squeeze your buttocks together. Rotate your arms in and out from the shoulders, then let them lie at your sides with palms facing up.

PELVIC BOUNCES

This is a wonderfully expressive exercise to awaken the energy at the base of the spine. The more energy you release as you practice the exercise, the more orgasmic it can become. After this exercise, relax in the Corpse Posture (see page 61).

1 Lie on your back with knees bent, feet flat, and a pillow or cushion under your buttocks.

2 Inhale and raise your pelvis from the pillow, then exhale audibly and bounce your pelvis back on the pillow. Repeat several times.

SINGLE-LEG FORWARD BENDS

This posture massages the abdominal organs and helps stretch and lengthen the spine. Practice it first with your left leg extended and then with your right. To come out of it, inhale and run your hands slowly up your legs, straightening your spine.

1 Sit on the floor with the sole of your right foot on the inside of your left thigh. Link your thumbs together, then inhale, hold your breath, and reach forward then upward.

2 Exhale and fold forward from the waist, bending from the base of the spine and reaching toward the toes of your left leg. Relax your head and neck and take deep breaths.

FORWARD BENDS

The aim of this exercise is to stretch your spine along the length of your leg. For some, this may seem impossible, and there is always a temptation to fight with your body in a desperate attempt to reach your toes. Keep your legs straight, and if you can't reach your toes, give up the fight and just rest your hands on your legs and, as you breathe, allow your body, head, and neck to relax. With practice, you will probably soon be able to reach your toes. To come out of the posture, inhale and run your hands up your legs slowly while straightening your spine.

1 Sit on the floor with your spine straight and legs stretched out in front of you. Link your thumbs together and rest your hands on your knees, then inhale. Hold the breath, reach toward your toes, then stretch up and and lean back at an angle of about 10°.

2 Exhale and fold forward from the waist, holding your toes if you can reach them or your lower legs if you can't. Hold the position, taking slow, deep breaths and lowering your body to your legs with each exhalation.

THE INCLINED PLANE

This posture acts as a counter-stretch to the Forward Bends. To come out of it, exhale and sit on your buttocks, then gently lie down in the Corpse Posture (see page 61).

Sit on the floor, legs straight and feet together, and lean back on your hands. Keeping your legs straight, inhale and push down with your hands to lift your body off the floor.

SINGLE LEG RAISES

This exercise stretches your leg muscles and helps to strengthen your abdomen and lower back. As you practice it, focus your attention on your breath and keep your upper body as relaxed as possible.

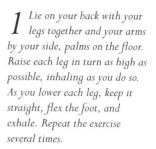

1 Lie on your back with your legs together and your arms by your side, palms on the floor. Raise each leg in turn as high as possible, inhaling as you do so. As you lower each leg, keep it straight, flex the foot, and exhale. Repeat the exercise several times.

2 As an easier variation of the exercise, again raise one leg at a time but keep the foot of the unraised leg flat on the floor.

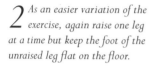

DOUBLE LEG RAISES

This is a demanding exercise, so take care not to strain your lower back. Raising both legs requires strong abdominal muscles, and if you find you need to support yourself, slide your hands, palms down, under your lower back close to your buttocks.

Lie on your back with your hands close to your buttocks, palms on the floor. Inhale as you raise both legs to an angle of about 45°, hold the breath and the posture, then exhale and lower your legs until they are just off the floor. Repeat as often as is comfortable.

THE COBRA POSTURE

This posture tones and massages the internal organs, improves circulation, and can help with menstrual pain and discomfort. To come down from it, exhale, then slowly and smoothly relax your arms. Repeat it as often as you can comfortably manage.

1 Lie face down with your legs together. Place your hands under your shoulders, palms on the floor, and rest your forehead on the floor.

2 Inhale, brush your nose and chin forward along the floor to lengthen your spine, then bend back to lift your chest as high as you can.

3 Push down on your hands to raise your chest further while keeping your shoulders down, head back, and legs flat on the floor.

4 Stretch further by straightening your arms. Take two or three deep breaths while holding the posture.

SHOULDER EXERCISE

This exercise helps to relieve tension in the shoulders. An alternative version is to bring your shoulders up to your ears as you inhale, hold them up as you exhale, and then let them drop.

1 Stand with your feet about 18 in (45 cm) apart and parallel. Inhale through your nose and lift both shoulders up to your ears.

2 Hold the breath and feel the tension, then exhale from your mouth and drop your shoulders down. Repeat several times, then gently roll your shoulders in both directions.

THE FISH

It is good to practice this after a Shoulderstand (see page 75) as it acts as a counter-stretch. To come out, relax your head then your hands and shoulders.

1 Lie on your back with your legs together, and place your palms on the floor beneath your thighs.

2 Inhale, push down on your arms, and arch your spine, resting the top of your head on the floor.

THE DOG POSTURE

This stretches the leg muscles and circulates energy. Visualize drawing energy from the earth up your arms, filling your heart center, then send it down your legs and back into the earth. To come out, exhale through your nose, bend your knees, and sit on your heels. Rest your forehead on the floor and bring your arms by your side with palms facing upward in the Child's Posture (see page 73).

1 Kneel with your legs together and toes curled under, then put your palms on the floor and straighten your arms. Exhale completely through your nose.

2 Take a complete breath in and, as you inhale, straighten your legs, taking care to distribute your weight evenly between your hands and feet and along the soles of your feet. Keeping your hands still, push your body toward your legs so that your hips form the apex of a triangle, and try to get your heels on the floor. Take deep breaths.

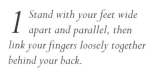

1 Stand with your feet wide apart and parallel, then link your fingers loosely together behind your back.

CHEST OPENER

As its name suggests, this posture stretches the front of the chest and opens out the airways within the lungs. To come out of it, inhale and then as you exhale, rest your arms on your back and slowly roll up. Release your arms and give your legs a shake.

2 Inhale through your nose, lean forward so that your body is parallel with the floor, and lift your arms as high as you can behind you.

3 Exhale and fold forward from the waist, keeping your arms raised and legs straight. Stay bent over for a few deep breaths, feeling your chest open and expand.

SIDESTRETCH

In this exercise, you put your arms above your head and lean alternately to the left and the right. As you do so, you will feel your sides being stretched and your spine flexing.

1 Stand with your feet apart and stretch both your arms up above your head close to your ears. Take hold of your right wrist with your left hand.

2 Inhale, stretch the right arm up, exhale, and lean to the left. Then inhale, straighten up, exhale, and lean to the right.

3 To come out of the posture, first inhale and at the same time stretch both arms forward then upward. Let your wrists relax and go limp.

4 Now hold your arms at shoulder height and relax your elbows and shoulders.

5 Finally, flop forward from the waist and let your wrists, elbows, head, neck, and shoulders relax completely.

THE HEADSTAND

Performing Headstands brings a multitude of benefits to both mind and body and, with regular practice, you will soon notice an improvement in your physical and mental fitness. The Headstand eases pressure on the lower back and can help with back problems. It also allows the heart to rest and helps to improve circulation, but women should avoid this posture when menstruating. Initially you will probably feel pressure on your head and neck, and you may find it helpful to visualize being held up by your ankles, which releases the pressure and keeps most of your body weight on your forearms. To come out of the posture, bend your knees, then lower them to your chest and put your feet on the floor.

1 To begin the exercise, kneel down, place your forearms on the floor, and clasp your elbows with your hands.

2 Keeping your elbows still, release your hands and link your fingers together, resting them on the floor.

3 Put your head on the floor, supporting the back of it with your interlaced fingers. Then inhale, and straighten your legs to lift your hips.

4 Slowly walk your feet toward your face until your hips are in a straight line over your spine.

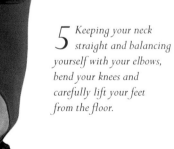

5 Keeping your neck straight and balancing yourself with your elbows, bend your knees and carefully lift your feet from the floor.

SUPPORTED HEADSTANDS

If you have never performed a Headstand before, or if it is a long time since you last tried one, you might find it easier at first to use a wall for support than to attempt a free-standing Headstand.

To do this, simply follow the instructions shown here, but kneel with your head and fingers close to the wall. Then, when you straighten your legs, you can rest your heels, your buttocks, or or the backs of your legs lightly against the wall for support and extra balance.

6 Give yourself time to balance then, using your abdominal muscles, lift your knees up gently, straightening your legs while keeping your feet relaxed. Give your body a chance to adapt and breathe very deeply.

THE KNEELING POSTURE

When you first practice this posture, use pillows to support your back to prevent difficulties with the stretch. Come out of it carefully, using your hands and arms as support before gently releasing your legs.

1 Begin by kneeling down with your knees apart. Then very gently ease yourself backward onto one elbow.

2 Now lean back on both elbows and carefully lower your shoulders toward the floor. If you are unused to this posture, put a pillow beneath your back before you begin to lean back.

3 Lie flat, shoulders and head on the floor, and feel your thighs, knees, and lower back being stretched. Bend your arms and hold onto each elbow.

1 Stand with your feet about 18 in (45 cm) apart, knees slightly bent. Put your hands on your hips, on your back, by your side, or up in the air.

2 Thrust your pelvis forward and backward, swing it from side to side, or move it in circles, making the movements progressively more distinct.

PELVIC THRUSTS

These exercises help activate the sacral chakra (see page 18) and release blocked energy. The movement is very sexual, so it is wonderful for giving expression to your sexuality. You and your partner could try it together, facing each other, keeping eye contact while moving your hips. Keep your jaw relaxed and mouth open, allowing any sounds to emerge. This will help you release inhibitions or express emotions.

The Camel Posture

This exercise stretches the entire front of the body and helps to strengthen the abdominal muscles and keep the spine flexible. To come out of the posture, exhale, sit back on your heels, and bring your body forward to rest in the Child's Posture. Stay quietly in this position for as long as you wish.

1 Kneel with your knees apart and toes touching. Inhale, and as you do so, push your hips forward and arch backward, clasping first the right then the left ankle while gently dropping your head back toward your feet.

2 While holding your ankles, take deep breaths, thrusting your body upward with each inhalation and relaxing it each time you exhale. Continue for as long as you comfortably can.

3 Adopt the Child's Posture by crouching in a kneeling position with your forehead resting on the floor. Put your arms by your sides with the palms of your hands upward.

THE BRIDGE POSTURE

This is a posture that helps to strengthen the lower back and abdominal muscles. There are a number of variations to this posture, but the one shown here is particularly good for beginners.

You should tuck your chin into your chest during this exercise to help activate the thyroid, a gland in the neck that produces hormones essential for the nervous system and the metabolism.

1 Lie on your back. Exhale, bend both knees into your chest, and hug your knees. Then hold the fronts of your ankles. By pulling against your ankles, with your feet flat and slightly apart, you can lift your back, buttocks, and hips clear of the floor.

2 Inhale, tilting your pelvis forward and up and lifting as high as you can. Breathe deeply and regularly and hold the posture as long as you can.

3 To come out, lower your spine, starting at the top and rolling downward. Bend your knees to your chest, then stretch your legs out on the floor.

SHOULDERSTAND AND PLOW

The Shoulderstand is an inverted posture that invigorates and rejuvenates the whole body. The Plow is an extension of it, created from it by bringing your feet back over your head to touch the floor.

1 Lie on your back on the floor with your legs together, arms by your side and palms facing downward. Inhale, and at the same time push down on your arms to lift your legs, hips, and thighs clear of the floor.

2 Exhale, straighten your legs, and support yourself with your hands, your thumbs at the front of your body and your fingers around the back.

3 To reach the Plow Posture, as you exhale, gently lower your feet to the ground behind your head, touching the floor with your toes if you can.

4 Stretch your arms above your head and hold onto your toes with your fingers.

NECK AND HEAD EXERCISES

These exercises will help to release tension in the muscles of your neck and shoulders. Tension in these muscles can be both the cause and the result of mental tension, and so you may find the exercises particularly beneficial at the end of a tiring day, or at any time when you are feeling under stress. You can do them either standing, sitting, or kneeling: the important thing is that you are comfortable, and you keep your spine straight and vertical. For maximum benefit, combine the exercises with deep, unhurried breathing, inhaling through your nose and exhaling through your mouth.

1 Face forward with your neck straight and inhale deeply, then exhale through your mouth, tilt your head back, and let your jaw drop open. Repeat this exercise several times, alternating it with allowing your head and neck to rest while taking deep, slow breaths with your jaw relaxed and your mouth slightly open.*

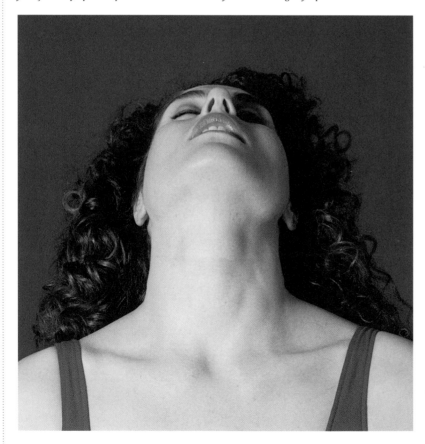

2 Check that your spine is straight and your shoulders level, then roll your head first to one side and then to the other.

3 Breathe in deeply, relax your shoulders, and then breathe out, dropping your chin to your chest to stretch your neck.

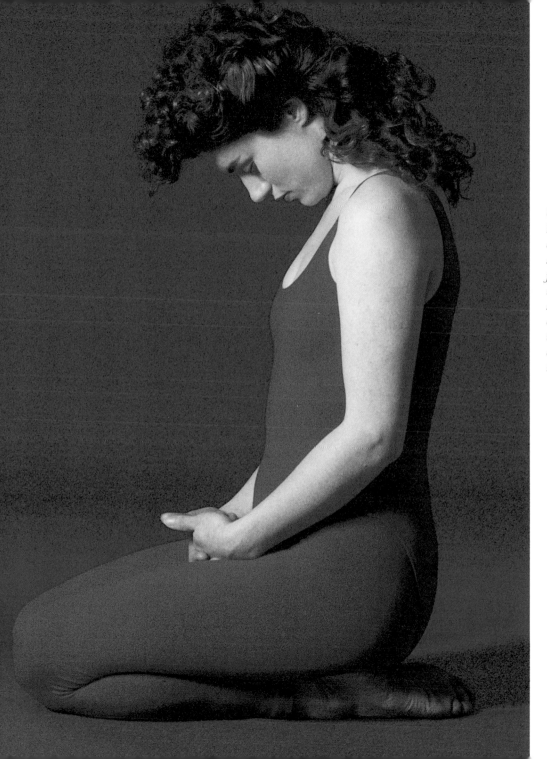

STRAIGHT SPINE

For the neck and head exercises, sit, kneel, or stand in a way that you find comfortable and relaxed. Keep your spine straight, and concentrate on exercising the muscles of your neck and shoulders and relaxing your jaw.

SOOTHING YOUR EYES

After exercising your eyes, rub the palms of your hands together quickly to generate some heat. Then cup your palms over your closed eyes and allow the darkness and warmth that this creates to soothe them. This treatment is also pleasant when your eyes are tired after a hard day's work.

FACE, JAWS, AND EYES

You can do these exercises almost anywhere. Those for the face help to release tension in the muscles of the face and jaws, and those for the eyes can help relieve eyestrain and may improve eyesight. Before you do the eye exercises, stretch one arm out in front of you with the thumb raised. Focus on your thumb for a few moments and then look as far beyond it as you can. Alternate between focusing on your thumb and focusing beyond it. At the end of the eye exercises, keep your eyes open and briefly roll your eyeballs up toward the top of your head, so that only the whites of your eyes are visible.

You can do these exercises in sequence, as shown here, starting with those for the face and jaws and finishing with those for the eyes. Alternatively, you can do any of the exercises on its own, or in combination with one or more of the others and in whatever order you prefer.

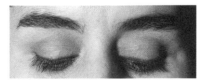

1 Keeping your mouth wide open by holding a wine cork between your teeth will stretch your jaw muscles and release tension in your face and neck.

2 Move your face and lower jaw using as many muscles as you can. Tighten the muscles by pursing your mouth, squeezing your eyes tight, and tensing your forehead.

3 Open your eyes as fully as you can, then open your mouth wide, stick your tongue out and down, and move it rhythmically from side to side.

4 Keep your head still and move your eyes around. Begin with clockwise circles, as if your eyes were following the path of the hands of a large clock.

5 After several clockwise circles of your eyes, make several anticlockwise and then alternately look up and down a few times, again without moving your head.

6 Finish by darting your eyes at random around your imaginary clock face for a while, and then look alternately left and right several times.

SLEEP

Sleeping is a natural, vital function that we generally take for granted. We spend about a third of our lives sleeping, but the length of time we are asleep is not as important as the quality of the sleep we get.

Most of us have had the experience of feeling completely unrested after a night's sleep, and the quality of our sleep is affected by a number of different factors. For instance, the cycles and forces of nature, and our sensitivity to them, have a very noticeable effect on our physical and mental energy and subtly influence our daily patterns, including our sleep patterns. A very basic example is that at the time of the full moon you may find that you have more energy than at the time of the new moon. Our mental and emotional conditions also affect our sleep, as do the polluted atmosphere of city life and its constant background noises.

PREPARING FOR SLEEP

Eating a large meal, or eating late at night, might induce sleep, but will most definitely have a negative effect on the quality of it. The body changes rhythm at night and cannot break down foods as easily as it can during the day, so any toxins in the undigested food will tend to clog the system. It is advisable to wait three or four hours after eating before sleeping, and, as far as possible, you should try to eat earlier in the day—before the sun goes down—when the digestive fire is stronger.

We also need to cleanse our minds of the worries of the day in order to prepare ourselves for sleep. Allowing the body to relax completely and the mind to switch off is not as easy as it sounds, which is why yoga and meditation are such valuable tools for freeing the mind of endless internal chatter. By using these techniques, you can learn to be in control of your mind and body, rather than letting them control you.

Making love is a wonderful way of releasing tension, clearing the mind, and restoring the body. Alternatively, share and exchange energy with your partner by just lying in bed together, holding each other, enjoying the smell and touch of each other, making love without having to have sex, then sharing sleep together.

To help yourself get the most out of your sleep, you can do simple exercises to relax your body and ease your mind. Lie on your back, on or in your bed, with your arms by your side and your palms facing up. Inhale, tense all your muscles in turn as tight as you can, feel the tension, hold it for a moment, then exhale with a sigh as you relax. Start with your toes and feet and work your way up your legs and body, tensing and relaxing each muscle group in turn, and finish with your facial muscles.

IV

MIND AND SPIRIT

Rest and Renewal

The ancient Taoists, by observing nature, noticed that things that moved slowly tended to live longer, and longevity was a Taoist obsession. Most of us do not give much thought to longevity, but the pace of modern life is so unhealthily fast that we can all benefit from slowing down and coming back to a natural, relaxed state of mind and body.

The often unrelenting pressures of daily life take their toll on us in many ways, physically, mentally, emotionally, spiritually, and sexually. One of the dangers of these pressures is that we are often unaware of just how much they are affecting us, sometimes until it is too late to take action to counteract them. But there are some simple steps that you can take, both alone and together with your partner, to protect your mind and body from overload, to free up the flow of inner energy, and to rejuvenate your sensuality. These steps include learning how to relax, finding inner peace through meditation, using reflexology to energize your vital organs, and creatively awakening your five senses and your imagination.

Stress and Tension

Stress and stress-related disorders are increasingly common in our society. We have also developed a sort of chronic impatience, a need for instant gratification that is reflected in phenomena such as a preference for "fast food" instead of a leisurely meal, and an ignorance of the joys of unhurried lovemaking. Sex has become a commodity. It is used to sell just about everything, and during the act of sex we tend to be racing to the finish rather than experiencing each glorious moment as it is happening. We need to learn about relaxation both in our daily routine and in our lovemaking.

One of the most common symptoms of stress is tension. This drains our energy resources, and causes physical ill health as well as tiredness and emotional imbalance, because our minds and bodies are intimately linked. If you feel anxious, then your body tenses, but if your mind is relaxed, your body will be relaxed.

We hold tension in different areas of our bodies, such as the muscles of the shoulders, neck, jaw, and face. Many people are unaware of this and spend their lives, even

> **"The multiple colors blind the eyes, the multiple sounds deafen the ears."**
>
> LAO TZU

while sleeping, in a state of physical and mental tension. It is very important that we regularly take time out to relax our minds, because we are so constantly bombarded by external stimuli that we need to switch off and make some inner space for ourselves. Yoga and meditation can also help you to relax, and these are themselves improved if you can relax before you practice them.

RELAXATION TECHNIQUES

When you are able to relax completely, your whole being is refreshed and rejuvenated. A few minutes of deep relaxation can actually be more beneficial than hours of restless sleep, whatever your age or occupation. But you need to be truly relaxed—a night in front of the television, for example, relaxes neither the body nor the mind; in fact, it drains your mental and physical energy even more.

RELEASING TENSION
Relaxation is best carried out when you are lying flat on your back, but you can also do it in a chair if it makes you feel more comfortable. To relax lying down, the Corpse Posture (see page 61) is an ideal posture. Once in the posture, you can systematically isolate, tense, and then relax each muscle group in your body, from your toes to your head. When you have done that, you will know what tension feels like in each part of your body, and how to release it.

When you have relaxed all your muscles, concentrate on your breath. Finding a steady rhythm and breathing slowly and deeply will help you to relax your mind. Close your eyes and detach yourself, become a witness to your mind and body and, as you relax, imagine the weight of your body pressing into the earth, completely supported, safe, and nourished. Just let go completely, and allow your body to relax and your mind to float free. To help you clear your mind of intrusive thoughts, try focusing it on a single image, such as an imaginary pinpoint of light.

As the muscular tension is released and your mind becomes calm, your entire system will slow down. Even after just a few minutes of deep relaxation (allow yourself 20 minutes or more in total) you will feel refreshed and rejuvenated, with peace of mind and a new-found vitality.

RELAXATION AND LOVEMAKING
Calm and relaxed is the ideal state to be in for practicing yoga and meditation—and for lovemaking! It makes everything better, because your senses awaken and the desire to rush to climax is replaced by a wish to appreciate and savor every moment as it happens. Practice deep relaxation with your partner and enjoy the euphoric energy that it induces, and with calm, clear minds and relaxed bodies your lovemaking will enter another world.

MEDITATION

*Meditation, which is not about doing but about being,
is time you give yourself to be alone and undisturbed, with your mind still
and focused. The inner tranquility that this produces brings
spiritual nourishment, joy, and wisdom.*

Meditation is one of the most important branches of yoga (see page 48) and, just as the asanas are used to bring physical health and suppleness, it is used to promote mental and spiritual well-being. There are many different meditation techniques, including using mantras both silently and out loud (see page 21), focusing on an image or symbol, or simply following your breath as it moves in and out. Meditation techniques can be taught, but a state of meditation cannot be forced: it happens by itself, when it is ready, and the experience of it is unique to each individual.

ENJOYMENT
Stilling the mind from ceaseless chatter and thoughts, and giving yourself the time and space to travel inward, to your own inner universe, brings its own rewards and can be infinitely enjoyable.

I used to regard my daily meditation practice as one of my disciplines, along with yoga. This made it a struggle for me, because I was always looking for some reason or excuse not to do my meditation practice, and then I would inevitably feel guilty about missing it.

One day, however, I lit a candle, sat down, and closed my eyes. I followed my breath and mentally watched thoughts drift in and out of my mind without becoming attached to any of them. For the first time, I was experiencing "being in" meditation, rather than "doing" meditation. For me, that was the key, and meditation is now a daily ritual that puts a smile on my face, a song in my heart, and peace in my mind.

TIME FOR YOURSELF
You should regard meditation as an opportunity to refresh and revitalize your being. It is time you set aside for yourself without intrusions, and can be a liberating experience of self-discovery.

Meditation also has important and beneficial physiological and psychological effects—oxygen intake increases, the heart rate decreases, blood pressure drops, the body rests, and the mind is cleansed.

No effort is involved in meditation, and it does not require concentration. You just have to be there for it and open yourself to receive it. Each of us has the capacity to do so: we don't need to look outside ourselves, we just need to be within.

MEDITATION EXERCISES

To develop your ability to meditate, set aside about 20 minutes a day to practice. Unplug the phone, turn off the television, stereo, or radio, and find a comfortable place in your home where you enjoy sitting. Your body temperature will drop as you relax, so make sure the room is warm. If necessary, have a blanket or shawl handy to wrap yourself in.

With your spine held comfortably straight, sit cross-legged on the floor or sit on the edge of a chair with your feet flat on the floor. Yogis adopt the *Padmasana* or Lotus Posture, which is ideal for meditation as it provides a balanced position in which there is a triangular path for the flow of prana (see page 16). Rest your hands on your legs with palms facing up and adopt a *mudra*—a hand gesture, such as forming a circle with the index finger and thumb of each hand—to channel subtle energies.

BREATHING

Take deep breaths to regulate your breathing, and find your own rhythm. Close your eyes and, breathing in and out through your nose, follow the course of your breath. If thoughts enter your mind, just watch them float in and out and focus on your breathing. Remember, there is no effort involved in meditation—just allow yourself to be.

USING A CANDLE

Sit comfortably on the floor or on a chair. Light a candle and place it in front of you. Close your eyes, breathe deeply in and out through your nose, and then slowly open your eyes and focus on the candle flame. Then, when you are ready, close your eyes and breathe deeply.

To help you tune in to the energy patterns and flow within your subtle body, focus your mind on each of your seven chakras in turn, starting at the base chakra. Visualize each one in its appropriate color and, at the same time, repeat the mantra associated with it, either silently or out loud (see page 19).

THE INNER SMILE

Sit comfortably and close your eyes. Turn the corners of your mouth up, then mentally transport this "smile" into your body and direct it to your internal organs. Visualize them smiling back at you. Giving your organs positive energy and showing gratitude for the work they do is part of honoring yourself.

FOCUSING ON THE CHAKRAS
Placing your hands over the area of each chakra when you meditate on it will help you to concentrate on it and reinforce the flow of energy through it.

REFLEXOLOGY

According to the theory of reflexology, our feet, hands, and sexual organs are richly endowed with nerve endings and energy meridians that connect with the major organs of the body. When pressure is applied to these nerves and meridians, the organs that are connected to them are stimulated and energized.

In traditional Chinese acupuncture, the body is viewed as having a network of meridian lines, or energy channels, close to the skin. These lines extend throughout the body from head to toe, and carry energy that harmonizes and activates the major organs, glands, and nerves. They are categorized as Yin when energy flows upward through them, and Yang when the flow of energy is downward.

Modern reflexology is more concerned with the flow of energy from nerve endings close to the skin's surface and also connected to the major organs. When pressure is applied to specific areas of the hands and feet—the reflexology points—the functions of the organs connected to those areas are stimulated and energized.

Gentle but firm pressure applied to the relevant zones of the hands and feet can also bring about healing by correcting imbalances and releasing constrictions in the energy flow to the internal organs and glands. If the receiver experiences pain in areas of the hands or feet where pressure is being applied, it normally indicates that there is a blockage or imbalance in the organ corresponding to that area. Gentle, concentrated massage will help to release the constriction. More general hand and foot massage can help relaxation, stimulate circulation, and increase vitality.

FEET AND HANDS

Washing and massaging your partner's feet (see page 107) is relaxing and energizing for both of you. It also harmonizes your moods and is a perfect preparation for lovemaking. Wash your partner's feet in warm water and, after drying, anoint them with oil or cream. The hands and arms are directly connected to the heart, so as you massage, direct the energy from your heart through your hands to your lover. Finger pressure, stroking, brushing, and sucking the toes are soothing and sensually stimulating experiences for both the giver and receiver. Give equal time and attention to both feet, including the top of the foot, the toes, the soles, the heels, and Achilles' tendons, massaging with a cream or a vegetable-based oil (see page 103).

When massaging hands, again give equal attention to both, including the wrists, and use a cream or oil. Massage the palms and thumbs, each knuckle and finger, including the tips and the webbing between each finger. Link fingers with your partner, palm to palm, and gently rotate the hand to massage the wrist, then lightly stroke the palm, wrist, and inner arm. It is easy to massage your own hands, and you can give yourself foot reflexology by walking barefoot on uneven natural surfaces.

GENITALS

The genitals also have reflexology points, and these are stimulated and massaged during intercourse and self-pleasuring (see page 141). In the Tantric and Taoist teachings on sex, specific postures are designed for circulating sexual energy through the body. The reflexology points on the hands and feet are also used during lovemaking to channel and circulate the energy. You can enhance the effect by using bandhas (see page 55) to retain outward-flowing energy that would otherwise be lost.

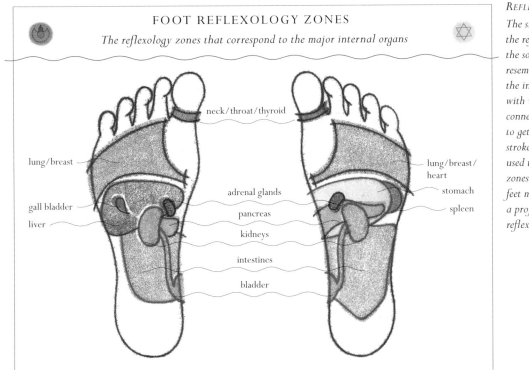

FOOT REFLEXOLOGY ZONES

The reflexology zones that correspond to the major internal organs

neck/throat/thyroid

lung/breast

lung/breast/heart

adrenal glands

stomach

gall bladder

pancreas

spleen

liver

kidneys

intestines

bladder

REFLEXOLOGY ZONES
The shapes of most of the reflexology zones on the soles of the feet resemble those of the internal organs with which they are connected. A good way to get an idea of the strokes and movements used to stimulate these zones is to have your feet massaged by a professional reflexologist.

Awakening the Senses

The Prana Upanishad, *an early Hindu scripture, states that the body is held together and supported through life by the five elements: earth, water, fire, air, and space, or* akasa. *Each element dominates one of our senses—the sense of smell is dominated by earth, taste by water, sight by fire, touch by air, and sound by space.*

As well as their connections with the five senses, the elements, or *tattvas,* are each associated with a particular chakra (see page 19). Earth is associated with the base chakra, water with the sacral chakra, fire with the solar plexus, air with the heart, and akasa with the throat. The brow and crown chakras usually have no element assigned to them.

Each element has its own symbol and color, and its own taste. Fire, for instance, is represented by a red triangle and is pungent and hot, and air is symbolized by a green oval and has an astringent taste. Other characteristics of the elements include the desires they are said to provoke or govern and the activities they are thought to favor.

A system of elements—the Five Elemental Activities—also features in Taoist traditions, but the elements are different and have different attributes. The five Taoist elements are wood, fire, earth, metal, and water, and they are each associated with specific senses and parts of the body. Earth, for instance, is associated with the sense of taste and with the spleen and stomach. Its other associations include saliva, obsession, humid weather, midsummer, and the color yellow.

Metal's associations include the sense of smell, the lungs and the large intestine, mucus, dry weather, autumn, and the color white.

SEX AND THE ELEMENTS

In the Tantric view, the five elements are created in the body during lovemaking, and texts of Oriental medicine state that sexual secretions change according to the dominance of a particular element.

From harmonization of the male and female, the elements are produced, evolved, then emerge: through our sexual organs we experience earth, the secretions that flow are water, the fire is kindled by the friction and passion of lovemaking, the air emerges from the movements, and space from ecstatic bliss. Through lovemaking, and enjoyment and appreciation of all the senses, the elements become balanced and harmonized—the female water element, Yin, cools the male fire of Yang, creating the potential for life.

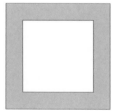

EARTH
shape: **square**
color: **yellow**
chakra: **base**
taste: **sweet**
desire: **survival**
activity: **collecting**
nature: **stable**

Sensory stimulation

Our senses are, however, easily dulled and need to be awakened from time to time, and arousing your partner's senses from a deep, dull state can be a liberating sensory adventure for both of you. Use your imagination to treat your partner to new aspects of sensory delight, encouraging him or her to try familiar experiences in unfamiliar ways.

For example, by blindfolding the eyes you are shutting off one sense, and this will help to enliven the others. We eat with our eyes first, so we can experience food in a new way by being fed tasty morsels when we cannot see them.

Sensory stimulation exercises are designed to create a deeper sense of trust and intimacy between partners. The giver offers the receiver devoted attention while using imagination to awaken the senses of his or her partner. The aim is to balance and harmonize the five elements. Yogic texts advise using visualization and breath control, as well as contemplation of the color, shape, and taste linked to each element, to focus each element in the heart chakra, and then channel it into precise areas of the physical and subtle bodies.

The effectiveness of the exercises will be greatly enhanced if you make them into a ritual. Begin by preparing your space, decide which of you will be the giver and which the receiver (or take it in turns), and honor each other and the space as safe and sacred.

Water
shape: **crescent**
color: **white**
chakra: **sacral**
taste: **salty**
desire: **meeting**
activity: **peace**
nature: **cool**

Stimulation Exercises

Prepare a range of different foods and drinks, and use your hands or mouth to feed them to your partner. Let him or her experience the smell and texture of the food before tasting it, or teasingly brush it past his or her lips. Alternatively, blindfold your partner and hand him or her different objects to touch, taste, and smell.

Awaken your partner's sense of smell by tantalizing him or her with the scent of a fresh flower or the smell of incense. Waft fragrant oils and perfumes under his or her nose and notice the subtle effects that this creates—different essential oils (see page 103) create different types and depths of physical and emotional response.

To stimulate your partner's sense of hearing, first use your index fingers and thumbs to massage his or her ears, then nibble, lick, and suck them. Follow this by breathing and whispering softly into each ear, and then create different sounds in different areas of the room.

Finally, you should both practice some eye exercises (see page 79), then sit and look deep into each other's eyes, seeing each other as if for the first time. Notice the colors, shapes, space, light, and shadow, and absorb the details as if you were going to recreate them on canvas. Be aware of what it is you reflect to each other and how "seeing" makes you feel.

Fire
shape: **triangle**
color: **red**
chakra: **solar plexus**
taste: **hot, pungent**
desire: **achievement**
activity: **labor**
nature: **hot-headed**

AIR
shape: **oval**
color: **green**
chakra: **heart**
taste: **astringent**
desire: **movement**
activity: **tasks**
nature: **restless**

AKASA
shape: **abstract**
color: **violet**
chakra: **throat**
taste: **bitter**
desire: **solitude**
activity: **thoughts**
nature: **void**

As part of the process of awakening your senses, introduce an element of fun and playfulness into your relationship and explore different aspects of yourselves and each other. Give your imagination a free rein and let your creativity come into play. Begin by standing naked, facing each other without touching each other. Then stand closer together, still without touching, close your eyes, and give yourselves a moment to feel the energy between you as you breathe.

SMELL
Now keep your eyes closed and explore each other with your noses. Smell your partner's hair and temples, then the nape of the neck, the valley between the breasts, the armpits, the small of the back, the genitals, the area behind the knees, and the feet. Notice the subtle differences in skin odor from one area to the next, and the effects they have on you.

MOVEMENT AND SOUND
Next, stand opposite each other and, as precisely as possible, each take turns to mirror the movements, facial expressions, and breathing patterns of the other. Then move around each other, first on your feet and then on all fours. Express yourself through sound, but avoid speaking: pretend to be an animal, moving as it would, playing as it would, and then letting the sounds emerge.

Another exercise that can often be fun is to communicate with each other in "gobbledygook," using a made-up language to express your feelings of love and desire, and to describe how you would like to make love to each other.

Expressing yourself in this way can be very releasing, emotionally, and provides an opportunity for sharing emotions without being limited by words.

TASTE AND TOUCH
Experiment with using your tongue. Gently lick and taste different parts of your partner's body, including the face and limbs, and discover the differences in skin texture and taste from one part to another. Keep your actions playful and be sensitive to your partner's reactions.

Next, with your eyes closed or using a blindfold, use your sense of touch to explore your partner's body in minute detail. But do not give your partner a massage at this stage: save it for later, and use this tactile exploration as an opportunity to "see" your partner through your sense of touch. Use the sensitivity in your fingertips to trace the outline of your partner's lips, to brush the lashes on his or her eyes, and to feel the texture of the skin.

In all these games, be creative, let the child within you come out to play and, in an uninhibited and sensual way, imagine that you are experiencing the wonders of your senses for the first time.

V
....

PREPARING
FOR LOVE

SETTING THE SCENE

By preparing the space and harmonizing your moods with conscious, focused intent, you are charging the atmosphere and yourselves with an energy that is essential if you wish to enhance your experience of lovemaking. In creating the right mood you are opening yourselves to deepening bonds of trust, intimacy, and playfulness with one another.

For most of us, especially those of us who live in cities, the pace of life is very fast and we are constantly subjected to stress. We are also bombarded by unwanted outside stimuli. These separate us from nature and, in order to shut them out, our senses gradually become dulled. As a result of this stress and sensory degradation, lovemaking can become boring and routine, and we cease to enjoy it because we have no energy or enthusiasm.

If your lovemaking has become a chore, or unadventurous, or even nonexistent, the guidelines on the following pages will help you (and your partner) to rekindle the flames of passion. They will show you how to reconnect with your divine origins and discover your true selves, and how to turn your lovemaking into a whole body and mind experience, and to recognize that physical contact without penetration can be a stimulating and erotic experience.

PREPARING THE SPACE

Among the many differences between men and women is the way in which they respond to stimulation. In most cases, a man's strongest sexual stimulus is visual, but a woman is more likely to be stimulated by the setting and the ambience—the music, lighting, smells, and colors. But we are all affected by the quality of our environment , so in creating a sacred space for lovemaking you help to create the mood. Preparing your sacred space—whether it be a room in your house or apartment or a natural outdoor space—becomes a preparation for an act of ritual lovemaking, worship, and devotion in which you can honor your divine origin and inner divinity.

The conscious act of preparing your space will protect it, cleanse it, and purify it. The atmosphere within it will also become charged with positive energy that you and your partner can absorb and transform during lovemaking.

> **"The application of proper means may be said to be the way of gaining all our ends."** KAMA SUTRA

PREPARING YOUR BODIES

Choose a time for your lovemaking, and your preparation for it, when you can be sure of no disturbance and when your energy is in balance and harmony with that of your partner. After preparing the space, you and your partner can arouse your senses and stimulate your subtle bodies (see page 16) by means of outer manifestations of your feelings for each other. These manifestations can include such activities as body ornamentation, dancing, bathing, and massage, which will prepare you physically, emotionally, and psychologically for liberation through sexual ecstasy.

By the use of ritual practices, you can elevate the mundane into the spiritual with awareness and creativity, activating mutual feelings of love and playfulness. This will give you the opportunity to forget who you are, to discard the various roles that make up your human existence, and to make room for the god and goddess within you to emerge.

BATHING AND MASSAGE

Taking a bath together, and washing each other, can be made into a ritual act of cleansing and purification. The bath can be warm and luxurious, with scented oils and a soap that creates a rich lather, or you might prefer bathing in cold water, which has the effect of vitalizing and toning the body and mind.

Giving and receiving a massage as a preparation for lovemaking allows you to explore and caress every inch of your partner's body and to honor its physical form. Prepare a sensuous massage oil (see page 103) and anoint your partner with it, then use the touch of your hands to awaken and relax his or her body and to harmonize your energies. When you have massaged your partner, exchange roles so that you are the one receiving the massage.

USING CREATIVITY

You can greatly enhance your lovemaking by creative playacting, dressing up, ornamenting your faces and bodies, and dancing and singing. Use your imaginations to become the living god and goddess within you (see page 96), deities dancing together for each other and expressing erotic sentiment and desire through gesture and movement. This will free your vital energies and allow them to circulate in your bodies, increasing your feelings of intimacy and harmonizing your moods.

Each of us has the potential to tap into his or her imagination and use it in preparation for the ultimate creative act. When you see one another as the most beautiful god and goddess in a universe of your creation, your coming together will be a celebration and honoring of the eternal female and male principles. Setting the scene is the ultimate foreplay, awakening the senses, body, and mind to new experiences. There is no rush, and patience in foreplay brings its own rewards.

LOVEMAKING RITUALS

Although most us of give them little thought, rituals are part of everyday life and range from the commonplace, such as getting dressed, to the more singular rites of birth, death, and marriage. Through ritual an act becomes focused, so when your lovemaking is made into a ritual, it takes on the power to increase spiritual awareness, offering you the potential to experience timelessness, egolessness, and oneness with the universe.

A ritual is not so much what you do but the intention behind it: if you perform any act consciously and with awareness, it becomes a ritual. The use of ritual was, and remains, a vital aspect of my Tantric training and it has become a part of my daily life, opening me to the reality of every moment being sacred and a celebration of being alive.

Sexual rites and rituals exist in many ancient traditions and are used for a variety of purposes. For example, some rituals are used for the release of emotions, to allow the transformation and release of any unwanted aspects of our nature. Ritual can be used as an outlet for these negative energies and as a means of balancing the inner masculine and feminine energies.

Energy flows in and out and around us. We are not separate from it, we are a part of it, and when any act is given attention in a focused way, as it is during a ritual, it connects us with energy in a way that heightens perception. Using ritual offers you and your partner the opportunity to express the hidden or repressed aspects of your nature in a safe and sacred space. It will help you to balance the energies within and between you and create mutual trust and a sense of the sacred.

For Tantrists and Taoists, ritual lovemaking was considered central to achieving freedom or enlightenment through self-realization, and we can borrow many elements from these ancient rituals and incorporate them into our lovemaking today. Bathing, yoga, breathing, massage, meditation, exchanging energy, and creating a sacred space are all rituals that can prepare you for a new and vitalizing experience of lovemaking.

By using ritual in lovemaking, you are honoring different aspects of yourself and your lover in a ceremonious way. Part of this involves surrendering yourselves to experience the divinities within you, transcending your personality and physical existence to experience the play of energy in the subtle body, using your bodies and sex as the vehicles for transformation.

PLANNING YOUR RITUAL

Ritual lovemaking works best when it is planned in advance. Choose a date and time for it when you can be alone and undisturbed, then begin to tune into each other's energy at least 48 hours in advance, for instance by doing your yoga and meditation practice together, and eating the same foods.

Hindu texts advise that the most potent times for ritual lovemaking are on the full moon or at the winter or summer solstice (but beware of overstimulation, because energy levels are high at these times). They also suggest that the best times to make love are between 7 p.m. and 12 midnight and again between midnight and 2 a.m.

PERFORMING YOUR RITUAL

Using ritual in your lovemaking can be fun and playful and is a wonderful way to celebrate making love to someone for the first time, or to revitalize a long-standing relationship. Use the following suggestions as a framework for your ritual, or invent your own: a ritual does not necessarily need a specific form, so just be creative, be natural, and enjoy yourselves!

After having prepared your sacred space (see page 100), bathe together and symbolically wash away any negativity or unwanted energy from your physical and subtle bodies. Then the man should anoint his Shakti (see page 14) liberally on different parts of her body with perfumed oils such as jasmine, rose, sandalwood, and musk. This helps to stimulate her base chakra (see page 19), whose element, earth, is associated with the sense of smell.

Next, you could paint each other's face, or the man might simply place a red dot between his Shakti's eyebrows to mark and promote the opening of her "third eye." Then sit facing each other, link hands and breathe together, and feel the energy circulating between you through your touching hands. Let your breathing become a gentle hum, or choose a mantra and repeat it out loud or silently.

The man can then ritually touch and kiss or use sound to vibrate different parts of his Shakti's body, and she can perform a ritual dance for her Shiva (see page 14), using it as a form of erotic and sensual initiation to an elevated plane of transcendence. You might then choose to exchange ritual gifts or make a verbal declaration to one another. Take your time, savoring every moment and seeing and touching your lover as if for the very first time. Eventually when Shakti is ready to receive her Shiva, he should honor her body as a sacred temple and ask permission before he enters.

You are now the god and goddess reigning in the heaven you have created in your sacred space, free of mortal cares, fears, and doubts, and experiencing the divine union of Shiva and Shakti.

THE DEITIES WITHIN

By worshiping the god and goddess within each other, you and your partner are honoring and awakening the divinity within yourselves. Honor the eternal female principle as embodied by the man and the eternal male principle as embodied by the woman, knowing that you meet yourselves in one another.

Whatever form it takes, worship helps to focus the mind, aids the channeling of energy (see page 128), and reminds the worshiper of his or her divine origin. Lovemaking becomes a sacred act, an act of worship, when you see the body as a holy temple, a place to reconnect with your original nature and your true self.

Imagine your partner is a living god or goddess. How do you behave in his or her divine presence? How do you make love to a god or goddess? How do you offer to be his or her servant? The answer is to be spontaneous and give freely from the heart—you are not meant to be bowing to the will of a superior being but acting with a genuine desire to love and to serve.

When you make love as an act of worship, close your eyes and forget who you are. Forget your face, your age, your history, your beliefs; forget where you are and let go of time. This act is your gift to yourself and your partner, so be completely natural and identify with your true nature—your divine aspect.

MANIFEST DEITIES

The first step is for each of you to bring out your god or goddess within. Use your imagination to create a fantasy setting in which to meet and unite with the mysterious inner stranger who holds the secrets of the art and mysteries of love, a place where together you experience eternity. Visualize yourself as the god or goddess, then make that deity manifest in your posture, your breath, and your expression. You can add to the effect by using clothing (try soft, natural fabrics draped around the body), jewelry, and cosmetics.

Open your eyes wide to connect with the god or goddess that your partner has become, as if meeting him or her for the first time. Then lovingly admire, touch, and caress different parts of each other's body as an act of devotion and honoring.

Be creative, play, and have fun. Think of each other's body shape as a yantra (see page 129), explore and touch each other as an act of devotion and honoring, and let all your senses come alive in the presence of your divine partner.

FINDING YOUR TRUE SELVES

By expressing your divine aspects during your lovemaking, you and your partner can find your true selves and reveal them to each other.

Use gentle words or simple gestures to convey your love and respect for each other, such as holding your hands together as if in prayer, close to the heart. Bow your heads in a spirit of humility and gratitude, honoring and celebrating the divinity of each other.

SEXUAL MAGIC

As god and goddess you have unlimited potential to create sexual magic. Each of us has the potential to play or act out various sexual roles linked to every aspect of human emotion, and to express and embody different archetypes, or innate patterns of behaviour.

Role playing offers lovers the opportunity to act out all the archetypal roles embedded in the human psyche, which are often repressed and in need of expression. And with awareness, sensitivity, and conscious, focused intent, it is possible for the ecstatic experiences that it brings to provoke a heightened perception of the world and the many levels of existence.

This role playing can be a development of the visualization of the god or goddess within, making it an acting out of erotic scenarios that depict the interplay between your two deities. Or you and your partner can use role reversal to explore your inner polar opposites.

ROLE REVERSAL

Role reversal is a powerful way of tuning into and expressing your inner male or female energies. The woman can imagine the penis of her partner as her own and express her male qualities, playing the active role, while the man can tune into his feminine qualities and aspects, play the passive role, and let his partner take the lead. Experiment with playing out other roles unashamedly and uninhibitedly, but be sensitive to each other's energy and stay in harmony with one another while you are exchanging passive and active roles.

Playing out these roles prepares lovers for the original and ultimate divine union of the god and goddess, Shiva and Shakti (see page 14). Make your breathing the music and your movements the dance, let the natural expressions on your face be your ornamentation, the sweet juices of your body your perfume, and the taste of your lover a potent elixir.

Draw the energy from your base chakra, stirring the goddess Kundalini Shakti to rise and stimulate each chakra in turn until she reaches the crown (see page 20). Then experience the bliss of ecstasy vibrating in every cell of your being as the energy flows from the crown down the front of your body and back up your spine. Circulate, exchange, and transform your sexual energy, elevating it beyond the physical and into the mystical and spiritual. Strengthen your bonds of love, trust, and intimacy to reveal and share the innermost part of yourself.

BODY ORNAMENTATION

Using body ornamentation as a playful, imaginative game brings out the creativity inherent in each of us, and when used as a preparation for ritual lovemaking it can be a potent and stimulating experience.

Cosmetics, jewelry, body markings, tattoos, and piercing play significant roles in traditions and cultures worldwide, especially in sexual rituals when particular colors and styles of makeup depict specific sentiments and energies.

Try to use natural cosmetics and apply them with your fingers or a soft brush, working carefully and with concentration so that the act of ornamentation becomes a creative meditation. Use your imagination and artistry to transform your partner with beautiful designs or symbols, or simply use color to enhance facial features such as the eyes and mouth, and to decorate the area between the eyebrows, which corresponds to the "third eye" of awakened consciousness.

USING COLORS

Colors have the capacity to arouse different sentiments. Reds, for example, are arousing, yellows make you feel cheerful, blues and greens are calming, and violet stimulates the chakras and promotes spiritual awareness. Applying different colors of makeup or body paint to various parts of the body (or painting symbols on them) has an aesthetic and psychological quality that stimulates and concentrates the energy in those areas. Try decorating each other's navel, heart, breasts, nipples, throat, hands, and feet, and allow it to be a seductive and sensual experience, aesthetically pleasing, capturing the imagination, and adding intimacy and playfulness to the relationship.

The act of painting and being painted really can create exciting and stimulating sentiments, awakening you to a new vision of each other and making your relationship deeper and stronger.

JEWELRY

If body paints and cosmetics aren't readily available, or if one (or both) of you is unwilling to use them, ornament your naked bodies with decorative items such as flowers or carefully chosen jewelry. Jewelry and body ornaments draw the observer's eye to the decorated part of the body, so they can be used to highlight particular features such as the length and shape of the neck or the curve and movement of the hips.

Stimulate your partner's erotic feelings by decorating yourself with, for example, necklaces, headdresses, earrings, arm bracelets, ornamented belts, finger rings, toe rings, and ankle bracelets. Or choose a single piece that holds a special significance, cleanse it using a natural oil or purify it in sweet smelling incense smoke, and ask your partner to place it on you and share its potent magic.

DANCING

Dance is an art form closely related to the arts of love, a means of nonverbal communication, a rhythm that moves beyond spoken language to communicate through movements, gestures, and expressions. It is also a dynamic meditation capable of evoking and channeling emotions and has the potential to reveal and express parts of your physical and subtle being that lie deeply buried within you, awaiting their expression.

There are dances in each of us: a dance to express feelings and emotions, a dance to celebrate, a dance to captivate. As the body begins to release, so the psyche begins to unravel itself, and you no longer move in the dance—the dance moves you and your body takes over. Surrender to the passion, the sexuality, the initiation to another level of understanding, and to the truth.

In Tantra, lovemaking is a dance: your breath and the sounds of love are the music, your heartbeat the rhythm. For your lovemaking to move beyond the material and physical and into the realms of the spiritual, you need complete acceptance of yourself, free of inhibition, guilt, or shame, and dancing can help you to achieve that.

Choose music that reflects your state of mind, then try dancing specific parts of your body in turn, starting with your feet and moving up to your head. Let different parts of your body lead the dance, and dance them until they are free of tension. As you dance, let your face and jaw relax and breathe through your mouth.

You and your partner can dance for each other, one at a time, or dance together, or alternate between dancing for each other and dancing together. Another option is to dance facing each other and mirror each other's movements in turn.

Whatever way you choose to dance, use your movements to communicate subtle erotic energy and emotion. Make your dancing a form of non-contact foreplay and a ritual of release that strengthens your bonds of love.

EVOKING EROTICISM
Dancing is a creative form of expression in which the body movements can tell a story, express emotions, and evoke eroticism.

CREATING A SACRED SPACE

When preparing a sacred space for your ritual lovemaking, you should seek to create an environment that will inspire spirituality. Your space should become a "heaven on earth" in which you and your partner can worship the god and goddess aspects waiting to emerge from within you, and become one with each other.

TRANSFORMATION

Use your imagination, let your fantasies run wild, and transform your environment into a setting in which all your senses participate in natural harmony with your spirit. Pay attention to detail and arrange things so that you have easy access to delights that awaken your senses of smell, touch, hearing, taste, and sight.

Tidy the space, and clean it as meticulously as you would your own body. For lighting, replace electricity with candlelight, which flatters the skin tones and incorporates the element of fire into your ritual. Drape fabrics over all hard edges, have plenty of soft pillows or cushions handy to support your bodies comfortably in different positions, and make sure the room is warm enough to be naked in.

Prepare edible "treats" to offer to each other and to the god and goddess within— set out plates of fruits and other sensuous foods, fresh water to drink, and perhaps a glass or two of wine to share.

Decorate your space in colors that evoke the kind of mood you're after—reds, oranges, or purples for stimulation, dark blues and violets for relaxation, and green for healing. Carefully positioned mirrors will give an illusion of space, and add an extra eroticism to your lovemaking.

Incense, herbs, and oils—particularly sweet scents such as jasmine, rose, ylang-ylang, sandalwood, rosemary, lavender, amber, mandarin, and patchouli—have the capacity to soothe and stimulate both body and spirit, and are an essential part of Tantric ritual. Experiment with blending your own scented oils to invoke different moods, and try mixing essential oils with water and spraying the mixture into the room or onto the sheets and pillows. If you burn some sage or some sweet incense, you will purify and cleanse the space, give it psychic protection, and generate a harmonious atmosphere that lifts the heart and mind. Use fresh flowers to decorate the space or to make garlands for each other, or use them to caress your lover's naked body. Or be extravagant and strew the scented sheets with petals or make love on a carpet of flowers.

The ways in which you can create your sacred space are endless and the potential for enhancing the eroticism of your lovemaking is unlimited. Try to use natural, organic materials as far as possible, creating a safe and sacred environment that delights all the senses and creates an atmosphere that pleases the spirit, uplifts the heart, and elevates the mind.

USING FLOWERS
Float the heads of fresh, fragrant flowers in a bowl of water to perfume your sacred space.

BATHING

Bathing before intimacy can greatly improve your mental and physical state and thus enhance your lovemaking, leaving you free to explore each other's body knowing you are clean both physically and mentally. A hot bath will open the pores, allowing toxins to be expelled, and soothe tired, aching muscles.

Bathing is not, however, limited to water. In Taoism, the water bath is one of five bathing practices, the other four being air, sun, fire, and mud. Each benefits the mind and body in different ways. To take an air bath, simply remove all your clothes and let the air reach all parts of your body. It is a liberating experience to be naked and enjoy one's nudity.

For a sun bath you need sunlight, a powerful source of energy that can nourish our bodies. It is important to take great care not to overexpose one's skin, and luckily the sunlight need not be strong or direct to be beneficial. Your body will absorb sufficient energy from indirect sunlight in the shade of a tree or umbrella.

A fire bath is wonderful for healing. It can be used to ease tense, sore muscles, and to relieve pain from sprains, arthritis, and other disorders. A fire bath is not as dramatic as its name suggests, but you still must take great care. Pour some alcohol into a small, fireproof dish, and light it. Use your hand to grasp the flame quickly and capture the heat, then open your hand over the part of your body that you want to heal, and let the heat escape from your hand onto your skin.

Mud baths cleanse the skin deeply and supply the body with minerals. Take a handful of mud or wet sand, and gently rub it over your body to stimulate your circulation and exfoliate the skin. Keep it simple and wash well afterward!

SENSUAL BATHING
Enhance the sensuality of your bathing by lighting the bathroom with candles and using a luxurious bath oil. Heating an essential oil in an oil burner will gently perfume the air.

SENSUAL MASSAGE

Massage is one of the arts of loving, and as well as being therapeutic and relaxing, it is a wonderful prelude to lovemaking. Massage can be a form of foreplay that gives you an opportunity to explore your partner's body and to experience touching all of it in a healing, relaxing, stimulating, and sensual way. It is a means of tuning in to your partner and harmonizing your energies to prepare you both for whatever follows.

TOUCH AND MASSAGE

We all need to be touched: it is a vital aspect of our lives, and our experience of it from the moment of birth onward has a profound effect on our physical and psychological development. Touch is a language, an intimate communication between the giver and receiver, and an important part of the art of loving. Some people find it difficult to receive touch, but trust and acceptance of it can be developed through sensitive massage.

Massage eases tension and releases blockages, allowing energy to circulate freely through the body and promoting good health, a calm mind, and a more fulfilling experience of sex. I think everyone should try having a professional massage. The sensations you experience help to put you in touch with your body, release built-up muscular tension, and give you an idea of the different strokes so you can use them with your partner.

GIVING AND RECEIVING

When you give your partner a massage, make it into a loving ritual, offer it as a gift to him or her, and remember that it can be just as pleasurable to give a massage as to receive one. The first step is to prepare the space and yourselves, and you should offer your partner the opportunity to take a warm, unhurried, relaxing bath while you get everything ready.

It is important to make the room a warm, comfortable environment, so that your partner can relax and will not feel cold while lying naked during the massage. The floor is probably the best place to give a massage, because it offers firm support and allows you easy access to the whole of your partner's body. To make it as comfortable as possible, create a mattress out of blankets covered with a sheet or towel to protect them from the massage oil.

Just before you begin the massage, light candles, and scent the room with incense or a few drops of essential oil mixed with water and sprayed with a plant sprayer.

During the massage, use your intuition to guide you to areas of your partner's body that are in particular need of attention, and make sure you give equal attention to both sides of the body.

If your partner is to get the most from the massage, it is important that he or she breathe slowly and deeply, exhaling the tension from his or her body as the strokes take effect, surrendering completely to the sensations that result, and expressing those sensations through appreciative sounds. These sounds will encourage you, because they demonstrate that your partner is enjoying the massage or receiving healing from it. In general, neither of you should talk during the massage. But if you have not massaged your partner before, it is a good idea to ask what parts of the body he or she would like you to massage and whether the pressure you are applying is too hard or too soft.

MASSAGE OILS

Using massage oil allows your hands to glide easily over your partner's body with smooth, clean strokes. Either use a ready-made massage oil or create your own by blending a few drops of an essential oil into a base oil, such as a vegetable oil, almond oil, or sweet almond oil. Experiment with different blends—for the essential oil, try lavender, ylang-ylang, rosemary, chamomile, patchouli, rose, cedarwood, or rosewood.

Gently warm the oil before use by standing the bottle in a bowl of warm water, and make sure your hands are warm before you begin the massage. Pour about a teaspoonful of the oil into your hands and rub them together to spread it over them. Then use your hands to spread this oil on the area of your partner's skin that you are going to massage.

CANDLES, INCENSE, AND ESSENTIAL OILS Candles provide a softer, more romantic light than electric lamps, and scenting the air with incense adds an exotic touch. The aroma of essential oils has beneficial physical and psychological effects for both the giver and receiver of the massage.

MASSAGE STROKES

As the giver of a massage, it is important that you keep the strokes flowing and continuous. Always keep one or both hands touching your partner's body from the moment you begin the massage until the end. Experiment with different speeds and pressures, and find a rhythm that enables you to make the strokes flow from one movement to another.

There are a number of basic massage strokes, a few of which are shown here for you to try. Use your intuition and common sense to guide you when choosing which strokes to use on different parts of your partner's body—notice his or her reactions and adapt the type, speed, and pressure of your strokes accordingly.

It is important that you prepare yourself before beginning a massage. Take some deep breaths and bring the energy into your hands by shaking your arms and your fingers. Then open and close your fingers in a grasping action to open the energy centers in your hands. Finally, because the intention of the giver of a massage is as relevant as his or her skill, make your intention clear to yourself and communicate it through your hands to your partner. Make an invocation, either silently or out loud, asking the healing energy to flow through your hands to promote the well-being of your partner.

GLIDING STROKES
Using the palms of both hands, make long, gliding strokes following the curves and structure of your partner's body. Then move your hands in wide circles along the body in a spiral pattern. These strokes work particularly well on the torso (including the shoulders) and on the buttocks, and will also help to spread the massage oil evenly.

PERCUSSION

This is a stimulating form of massage that tones the skin and improves circulation. Using the edges of your hands (right) or your knuckles (far right), make a rapid succession of strokes so that your hands bounce lightly up and down on your partner's body.

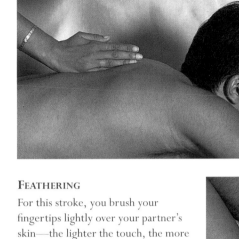

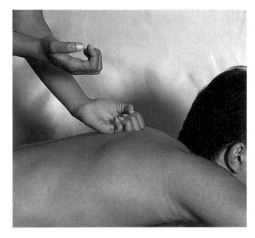

FEATHERING

For this stroke, you brush your fingertips lightly over your partner's skin—the lighter the touch, the more powerful the effect. With this stroke you are working on an energetic rather than a muscular level. It is a delightful all-over body experience and a gentle but stimulating way of concluding the massage.

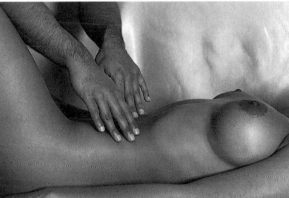

KNUCKLING

In this stroke, you press firmly but gently with your knuckles to relieve deep-seated muscular tension. Use this stroke on the fleshier parts of the body— it is particularly good on the buttocks.

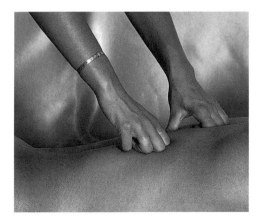

GIVING A MASSAGE

The basic sequence of a massage is to begin working on the back, covering the torso as a whole, then working on smaller areas—the shoulderblades, upper back, lower back, and buttocks, then along either side of the spine. (But do not apply pressure directly onto the spine at any time.) Now massage the back of each leg, first upward and then downward, and next massage each foot.

Then ask your partner to roll over, and massage his or her shoulders and neck. From there, work down each arm in turn, including the wrists, hands, and fingers, then gently work on the front of the torso, circling round the abdomen and up the sides with long, sweeping strokes, and massage the fronts of the legs. Now gently massage the scalp, face, and ears, then finish the session with long, sweeping body strokes, followed by feathering.

SHOULDERS AND BACK

First massage the whole of the torso several times from the shoulders down to the buttocks and back up again. Then concentrate your attention on individual areas such as the shoulderblades.

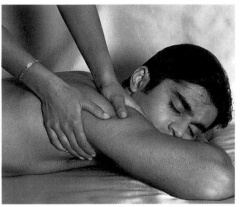

ARMS

With your partner lying on his or her back, massage down each arm in turn. Working down from the shoulder, concentrate on the fleshiest parts, such as the biceps. Finish working each arm by manipulating the wrist and massaging the hand.

HEAD

Massage firmly all over the scalp, using your fingertips, then work gently from the forehead down to the chin and outward from the center of the face to the sides.

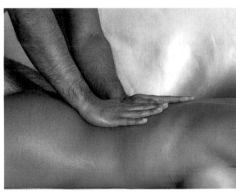

FINISHING STROKES

End the massage by connecting the entire body together again with long, sweeping strokes, followed by gentle feathering. Then, to complete the massage session, lightly rest your hands on your partner's body for a few moments to harmonize your energies.

FOOT MASSAGE

To give a foot massage, begin by pressing your knuckles firmly into the sole, covering it with small circling movements, then work over it again using your thumbs. Next, gently bend the toes back and forward, then massage the top of the foot with your thumbs before working on the grooves between the raised tendons. To do this, support the foot with one hand and run the tip of the thumb of the other hand firmly along each groove from ankle to toe. Do not, however, massage the ankle itself—you should always avoid massaging directly on top of a bone.

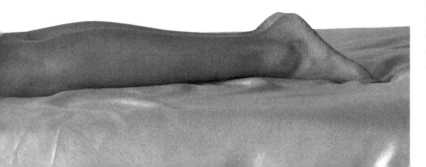

FOREPLAY

Lovemaking, like orgasm and ejaculation, should neither be forced nor rushed. If it is to be a truly satisfying and liberating experience, it is important that the moods and physical and subtle natures of both partners are in harmony. Gentle foreplay helps to achieve this.

Good foreplay also provides the preliminary sensual stimulation and arousal that most women need because, in general, they take longer to reach boiling point than men. And if a man is unable to satisfy his partner easily, the techniques of foreplay and of afterplay (see page 138) will help to improve his partner's response and balance and harmonize his and her different levels of excitement.

AROUSING A WOMAN

To arouse your female partner, begin by gently stroking and caressing her hair and head, then work down one side of her body, starting at her eyes. Kiss, lick, and gently breathe on and around her eyes, then move to her cheeks, mouth, ears, neck, shoulders, and breasts. The sensitivity of the breasts and nipples varies from one woman to another, but kissing, sucking, and gently caressing the breasts can arouse some women to high levels of excitement, causing the vaginal secretions to begin to flow.

Try using the tip of your tongue to circle around the nipple as if spiralling down and inward. From the breasts, kiss, lick, and caress her abdomen, then kiss and massage her feet and work up each leg in turn to her genitals. Stimulate her clitoris and vulva both orally (see page 112) and manually, but be sensitive to your partner's reactions because some women do not like manual stimulation.

Be imaginative and use different parts of your own body to massage and caress or stroke your lover's body. For instance, you could surprise her and make love to her hands with your mouth and tongue and fingers, enjoying a kind of safe oral sex. Often, a woman may indicate where she wants to be touched by directing her hand or eyes to the points of sensitivity. Watch her closely, then kiss or touch her on those points—you will know if you get it right.

This foreplay sequence should take at least 20 minutes and has the potential of arousing a woman to the fourth level of orgasm (see page 35).

AROUSING A MAN

For many men, gentle handling, licking, and sucking of the testicles and scrotum is extremely pleasurable, but when doing this, a woman must take care and be sensitive to her partner's response. In addition, some men can feel very uncomfortable about having their testicles touched, and you may have to allow your partner time to develop enough trust in you to let you touch and fondle him there.

Enjoy the sensation of complete body contact, using different parts of your body to stimulate his before handling his penis. The way in which you do this will depend partly on your own personal preferences and those of your partner, but you may have to take account of his sensitivity and level of excitement.

Touch his penis lightly or firmly along its whole length, or apply slight pressure at the root by encircling it with your thumb and index finger. Then lubricate the glans with saliva and gently feather and slide your fingers back and forward around it. After that, gently cup his testicles in one hand and, holding his penis with a firm but gentle grip, glide your hand smoothly up and down the shaft, changing the rhythm, speed, and pressure of the strokes in response to his reactions.

MUTUAL AROUSAL

During foreplay, take turns to give and receive pleasure and don't stop touching each other with your hands. Keep them moving over your partner's body and make head-to-toe body contact at as many points as possible. Tease and tantalize each other in a playful way by bringing each other to high levels of excitement before turning your attention to the genitals.

Do not concern yourself too much with technique: the important thing is to create and maintain arousal. And in order to experience the heights of Tantric bliss you have to accept yourself and everything in order to transcend and transmute it into spiritual liberation. Thinking too much about what you are doing will impede this process.

We all have the potential to experience our orgasmic natures, and to discover yours, you just need to let go, to "lose control" and be immersed in sensation. When you let your thinking mind give way to, and be guided by, your intuition, your body will take over and orgasm will become a whole-body experience.

GENTLE BEGINNINGS
Taking time to arouse each other allows you to express your love in many different ways, and will help you both to achieve true satisfaction.

KISSING

Kissing is an essential aspect of foreplay and helps contribute to the state of mind and receptivity to lovemaking. Tantric tradition teaches that a woman's upper lip is connected to her palate and clitoris and this subtle nerve channel has a special sensitivity. Sucking or gently nibbling the upper lip of a woman can be deeply erotic and sensual.

TECHNIQUES

Learning how to kiss is important. Different techniques, actions, and rhythms can be used on the mouth and on different parts of the body such as the nipples, penis, and vulva. When kissing on the mouth, both partners should drink from each other's lips and tongues with uninhibited relish, sharing and exchanging the vital, healing elixir of ecstasy. When you kiss be neither the giver nor receiver—try to "become" the kiss.

The secret of good kissing is to keep your face and mouth relaxed. This increases your sensitivity and enhances the pleasure of contact with your partner's mouth and tongue. A tense mouth creates empty space and poor contact with your partner's. The less empty space there is in your mouth when kissing, the greater will be your sensual, erotic pleasure.

The Taoists believe that the face and mouth reveal everything about a person's personality and sexual characteristics. For example, it is believed that the size and shape of a woman's vulva is reflected by the size and shape of her lips and mouth, and a man with thick, wide lips is said to have a big penis.

The mouth combines characteristics of both the penis (tongue) and the vulva (the mouth and lips), and the mucous membrane of the lips has a similar texture to that of the vulva. These characteristics provide partners with the opportunity to explore male and female qualities and exchange active and passive roles. Unlike the penis and vulva, however, the mouth and tongue are controlled by voluntary muscles. This gives us more control, so kissing can last for as long as you choose without tiring you, and passionate, erotic kissing can be as loving and exciting as making love, harmonizing the energy and sentiments of both partners.

TYPES OF KISS

Deep erotic kissing is given almost as much emphasis as lovemaking itself in the ancient Taoist texts. In many Eastern cultures, kissing is regarded as a deeply

SHARED INTIMACY
Kissing is a unique way of sharing and expressing intimacy, and a very erotic aspect of foreplay.

intimate part of lovemaking and rarely done in public. In other cultures, kissing is used to express different sentiments ranging from forms of greeting, an expression of tenderness, or an erotic exchange.

The *Kama Sutra* describes a number of different types of kisses. These include the Greatly Pressed Kiss, when the lower lip is pressed forcibly and touched with the tongue, and the Kiss of the Upper Lip, when the man kisses the upper lip of the woman while she kisses his lower lip. The Clasping Kiss is when one partner takes both lips of the other between his or her own lips, and the Fighting of the Tongue is when one partner uses his or her tongue to touch the teeth and palate of the other. The *Kama Sutra* also lists the parts of the body that are said to be particularly suited to kissing, including the forehead, eyes, cheeks, throat, breasts, lips, mouth, thighs, arms, navel, and penis.

STIMULATING THE SUBTLE BODY
The subtle body (see page 16) can be stimulated and awakened by using open-mouth contact on your partner's body, placing kisses with conscious intent on the areas of the seven chakras. In the Tantric tradition, kissing is known as "contact of the gates," and gazing into each other's eyes while exchanging passionate kisses harmonizes the energies and emotions of the couple.

The exchange of the subtle secretions produced by both partners during lovemaking is considered nourishing and vitalizing, and the Taoist texts suggest drinking as much as you possibly can from each other to harmonize the Yin and Yang within you both (see page 130).

This, like other styles of kissing, involves most of the senses—sight, taste, touch, and smell—so good oral hygiene is of extreme importance. It also calls for both of you to have a strong desire to share and exchange your special secretions, so it is something that can only be done with the right partner.

JADE SPRING
In the Taoist texts, the saliva of a sexually aroused woman is known as Jade Spring, and is considered the most precious of the three secretions produced by a woman (the other two being the White Snow produced from a woman's breasts and the Moon Flower Water released from the Palace of Yin, or womb).

Jade Spring is produced by ducts beneath a woman's tongue, and a Tantric technique is for the woman to place the tip of her tongue on the roof of her mouth as orgasm approaches, which is when the essence is produced. Then, as she climaxes, she offers her tongue to her partner to suck and drink the sweet, vital essences in the saliva, which are reputed to have great healing and medicinal properties.

In the Taoist texts on lovemaking, it is recommended that a man should swallow the Jade Spring to generate vital essence and strengthen his blood.

ORAL SEX

Genital kissing, licking, and sucking can be a very effective way of arousing your partner, provided you are both careful to ensure scrupulous oral and genital hygiene. The tongue has all the necessary attributes for erotic and sensual arousal and stimulation. It has the capacity to change size and shape, is warm and moist, and is able to move with deftness and strength in a variety of movements. And, according to Taoist tradition, energy can be directed into your partner's body through your tongue.

TONGUE EXERCISES

Exercising your tongue will help to strengthen it and give you a greater variety of controlled and sustained movement with which to thrill your partner. Incorporate tongue exercises into your yoga routine, or practice them with your partner in front of a mirror.

Begin simply by being aware of how your tongue sits in your mouth, and which parts of it are in touch with your teeth and your palate. Then just let your jaw relax, stretch your mouth wide open, and extend your tongue as far out and down as you can. Repeat this several times, then stick your lower jaw out as far as possible and stretch your tongue tip to reach the end of your nose. Now try stretching your tongue as far to the left and right as you can, then let it relax completely in a slightly open mouth. Next, rest your tongue on your lower lip, curl both sides up to form a tube shape, and breathe through it.

Sithali, a method of breathing with the tongue like this, is recommended for cooling the system, so it can be used during heated lovemaking or hot weather. It also helps to relieve hunger and thirst pangs. Inhale, drawing the air in through the tube created by your tongue, close your mouth, hold the breath, then exhale through your nose. Repeat five or ten times. If you cannot curl your tongue into a tube, let it rest on your lower lip and sip the air across the tip of it when you inhale.

Another useful exercise is to try rolling your tongue toward the back of your mouth, and to use the tip of your tongue to massage the floor of your mouth.

You will notice, while practicing these exercises, that you produce a lot of fresh saliva. If you exercise your tongue immediately before oral sex, you can use this saliva as a natural lubricant; otherwise, keep it in your mouth and then swallow it in one gulp. Within a few weeks of practicing these exercises, your oral dexterity and sensitivity should improve noticeably. You will become more aware of your tongue, and kissing will become less mechanical and more sensational.

FELLATIO

Vatsyayana, the author of the *Kama Sutra,* considered fellatio (kissing and sucking the penis) to be a special feature of the art of massage, and in the book he describes eight different ways of performing what he calls "mouth congress." He recommends that these be done one after the other.

The first is the "nominal congress," in which the penis is held in the hand, placed in the mouth, and moved between the lips; "biting the sides" is gently pressing the side of the penis with the lips and teeth. "Pressing outside" is kissing the end of the penis with closed lips, while "pressing inside" is when the penis is pushed a little way into the mouth, pressed by the lips, and then pulled out. "Kissing" is holding the penis in one hand and kissing it as if it were the lower lip of your lover; "rubbing" follows kissing, and consists of touching the penis all over with the tongue.

The last two actions are "sucking a mango," in which the penis is placed halfway in the mouth then forcefully kissed and sucked, and "swallowing up," when the penis is completely drawn into the mouth then pressed and sucked as if being swallowed.

CUNNILINGUS

In the ancient Eastern traditions, the vulva is considered the most sacred part of a woman's body. Tantrists honor the vulva as the Gateway to Life. It is the passage we all pass through in being born, and is also an entrance to both the past and the future. A man should think of his partner's vulva as the original location of Shakti, the source of life.

A good way to give your lover oral sex is to begin by kissing and caressing her face and body, working down slowly to her genitals (see page 108). When you reach her genitals, lovingly kiss and lick her pubic mound, then the outer lips of her vagina and her clitoris.

The clitoris is highly sensitive, and most women find that gentle stimulation with the lips and tongue is highly arousing. You should position yourself so that you can flick your tongue from side to side and upward along the lower side of the clitoral shaft, and then gently lick up on each side of it in turn. You could also try softly sucking the head of the clitoris between your lips, and lightly licking its head.

To vary the stimulation, move down from her clitoris to her perineum, the area between her vulva and her anus. This small area of skin is rich in nerve endings and in most women it is very sensitive to touch. Using the tip of your tongue, make light up-and-down strokes along the perineum, then either return to clitoral stimulation or turn your attention to her vulva.

Kiss the outer lips of her vulva (Hindu love texts recommend using mouth kissing to practice ways of kissing the vulva) and run your tongue along and between them. While you are doing this, you can increase the stimulation by darting your tongue in and out of her vagina. Start off with quick, shallow strokes, using just the tip of your tongue, and then make slower, deeper strokes with the whole of your tongue.

MUTUAL PLEASURE
For oral sex to be truly satisfying, it should be done in such a way that both partners find it enjoyable.

HOMOSEXUALITY

For homosexuals, as for heterosexuals, an inner balance of the male and female aspects, of Yin and Yang, is vital. Yoga techniques (see page 48), including meditation and breath control, can help to bring the body and mind into a state of harmony and balance.

Each individual has a different mixture and proportion of masculine and feminine traits on the spiritual, emotional, physical, and mental levels. And because male and female hormones exist in both men and women in varying proportions, in effect no man is completely male and no woman completely female.

With homosexual sex, it is impossible to experience the full balance of male and female energies and the highest harmony of Yin and Yang. However, homosexuality is not contrary to the Tao and in Tantric philosophy all variations of sexual intercourse have some positive and natural role in the fulfilment of human sexuality. The practices and techniques in this book can be used and adapted for homosexual couples of both sexes.

MALE HOMOSEXUALS

In both Tantric and Taoist texts, anal sex between men is considered unhealthy and potentially damaging for health and psychological reasons. It is thus considered necessary for male homosexuals to alternate active and receptive roles for health reasons and to balance the inner Yin and

Yang energies. One partner can stimulate his Yin energy, which is feminine and associated with water, by using meditation to focus his thoughts on water. In addition, massaging the penis will stimulate the reflexology zones (see page 141) that in heterosexuals are activated by the female partner's vagina during intercourse.

FEMALE HOMOSEXUALS

A man can easily massage the shaft and glans of his penis to stimulate the reflexology zones, but for homosexual women an even internal massage, stimulating all the zones, is not so easy.

Life force is needed if the body is to be energized through stimulating the reflexology zones. Sexual aids, such as dildos, have no vital energy, and the fingers, because of their size and shape, cannot provide balanced stimulation. However, one partner can stimulate her Yang energy, which is masculine and associated with fire and the sun, by sunbathing and thus absorbing the sun's energy into her body. Alternatively, she can use meditation to help her to direct her Yang energy to her genitals and ovaries.

VI

LOVEMAKING

LOVEMAKING POSTURES

By combining Tantric and Taoist sexual practices with an awareness of your bodies and how they function, you and your partner can achieve a new perspective on your lovemaking and turn it into a sublimely erotic and fulfilling experience.

To be aware, simply by reading this book, that there is more to sex than most people realize, and that the Tantrists and Taoists had the secrets of truly wonderful lovemaking, is the first step toward integrating these ancient wisdoms into your daily life. Even old, familiar ways of lovemaking can become new and exciting when you apply these techniques, and the joy and inner peace that this brings will enrich your life.

We all have favorite lovemaking postures, and every conceivable position of lovemaking has undoubtedly been tried by someone, somewhere, at some time or another. Whichever postures you choose, enjoyment of them can be greatly enhanced by developing an understanding of how your chakras (see page 18) are aligned with your partner's, your breathing patterns aid or hinder sensation, how the shape of a woman's external body can alter the shape of her vagina, and how

the softness or hardness of the thrusts will produce different effects. The trick is to have this awareness during lovemaking without actually thinking about it.

To help you to switch your mind off, either close your eyes and enjoy the sensations or look into your partner's eyes, and exhale through your mouth, freeing any sounds that want to come out.

Being comfortable when you make love is important, so have pillows available to support you in various positions. If your body is not used to any form of exercise, be gentle with it as you move and change postures. Meditation techniques and yoga practice can help you to prepare your mind and body for lovemaking.

My partner and I found that keeping a sense of humor is vital when you try some of the more demanding lovemaking postures. Although we have become much stronger and more supple from our yoga practice, we find that some of these postures are quite difficult to maintain. But whether or not you actually practice these postures doesn't matter—if nothing else, they illustrate that anything is possible!

"Passionate actions which arise during sexual intercourse cannot be defined, and are as irregular as dreams." KAMA SUTRA

OLD FAVORITES

This is the part of the book where the lovemaking postures that are described will be familiar to almost everyone. The postures depicted are some of the most straightforward of all lovemaking positions, but despite their simplicity they can be extremely satisfying for both partners. Most of us naturally assume these basic postures at some time or another during lovemaking, and with a little imagination you can easily devise your own variations on the basic themes and enjoy some playful experimentation.

Whenever you want to try something different, though, remember to communicate your desires to your partner, using words, movements, gestures, or sounds.

Intimate communication of this nature is particularly important in a long-term relationship, when lovemaking and the expression of sexuality often become limited to a relatively small range of unadventurous methods.

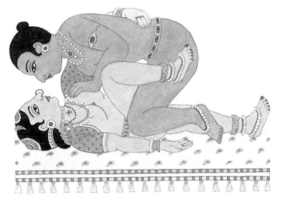

ADVANCED POSTURES

From my study of ancient Eastern erotic art, I think there is considerable evidence that the women depicted in the paintings and sculptures were highly adept at using their limbs and bodies to create the most extraordinary shapes and positions. They were, no doubt, well practiced in yoga.

Many of the lovemaking positions shown in these erotic images are described in love manuals such as the *Kama Sutra,* a Hindu work that was written some time around the second century A.D. by a sage called Vatsyayana. It includes a variety of information on sexual matters and describes numerous lovemaking postures. For those of you who are feeling adventur-

ous, I have described some of the more "gymnastic" of the *Kama Sutra* postures that were added to the Tantric tradition.

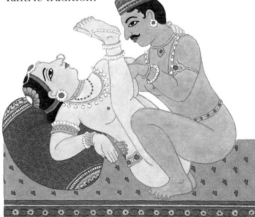

Rhythms of Love

The ancient love manuals contain useful advice on how the man should time and control his thrusting during lovemaking so as to maximize his pleasure and that of his partner. Many also describe the stages of a woman's sexual arousal and advise on how the man should respond.

The Nine Movements

SETS OF NINE

A Set of Nine consists of nine shallow thrusts and one deep, then eight shallow and two deep, followed by seven shallow and three deep and so on until you reach nine deep and one shallow:

1 nine shallow, one deep
2 eight shallow, two deep
3 seven shallow, three deep
4 six shallow, four deep
5 five shallow, five deep
6 four shallow, six deep
7 three shallow, seven deep
8 two shallow, eight deep
9 one shallow, nine deep

The aim is to go through as many Sets of Nine as possible without ejaculating. Men often find this amount of penile stimulation overwhelming at first, so it is important to vary the number of sets and the pace according to individual ability.

The *Kama Sutra* lists Nine Movements of the Man (see opposite), which should be performed during lovemaking with awareness and as artistically as possible. Making these movements gives the man the opportunity to observe his partner and her preferences during different stages of lovemaking. The *Kama Sutra* states that he should focus his attention on the parts of a woman's body on which she turns her eyes, and be aware of her sounds and actions during lovemaking, which reveal her level of excitement and pleasure. It is also possible for the woman to assume the male role and to use these different movements on her partner.

The Ten Stages

The Plain Girl, Su Nü, is also known as the Goddess of the Shell and is one of the triad of sex initiators of the Yellow Emperor in ancient Chinese tradition. She lists Ten Stages of Loving (see opposite), which describe a woman's movements during lovemaking and explain how these show the level of her passion and excitement, where she wishes to be touched, and the way she wants her man to move.

Nine Shallow, One Deep

The most popular thrusting method in the Taoist texts is based on the number nine, a number thought to represent powerful Yang energy. The rhythm—nine shallow strokes and one deep stroke—heightens pleasure, prevents early ejaculation, and maintains a high level of awareness and concentration; women find it delightful. The deep stroke, besides its sensory stimulation, forces air out of the vagina. This creates a partial vacuum within the vagina during the shallow thrusts, making the woman feel first tantalized then satisfied.

The man thrusts slowly, gently, and lovingly. For the first nine strokes, he allows only the head of his penis to penetrate his partner's vagina; on the following stroke, he allows the entire penis to penetrate. While thrusting, he should never withdraw completely.

THE NINE MOVEMENTS OF THE MAN

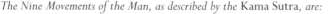
The Nine Movements of the Man, as described by the Kama Sutra, *are:*

1 Moving Forward—"When the organs are brought together properly and directly."

2 Churning—"When the lingam [penis] is held with the hand, and turned all round in the yoni [vulva]."

3 Piercing—"When the yoni is lowered, and the upper part of it is struck with the lingam."

4 Rubbing—"When the same thing is done on the lower part of the yoni."

5 Pressing—"When the yoni is pressed by the lingam for a long time."

6 Giving a Blow—"When the lingam is removed to some distance from the yoni, and then forcibly strikes it."

7 Blow of a Boar—"When only part of the yoni is rubbed with the lingam."

8 Blow of a Bull—"When both sides of the yoni are rubbed in this way, it is called the blow of a bull."

9 Sporting of a Sparrow—"When the lingam is moved up and down frequently, and without being taken out. This takes place at the end of congress."

THE TEN STAGES OF LOVING

According to the Plain Girl, the Ten Stages of Loving that a woman goes through are:

1 She holds her man tight with both hands, indicating that she wants closer body contact.

2 She raises her legs, showing that she wants clitoral stimulation.

3 She extends her abdomen, which shows that she wants shallower thrusts.

4 She moves her thighs, showing that she is greatly pleased.

5 She pulls the man closer with her feet, to show that she wants deeper thrusts.

6 She crosses her legs over his back, indicating that she wants more.

7 She shakes from side to side, showing that she wants her man to make deep thrusts on each side.

8 She lifts her body, showing that she is enjoying it extremely.

9 She relaxes her body, indicating that her body and limbs are pacified.

10 Her vulva floods, her tide of Yin has come. She is happy.

OLD FAVORITES

These familiar postures take on a new lease of life when each of you feels free and uninhibited. Let go of any dislikes you may have about your physical bodies, and turn your lovemaking into an act of worship where the personality is lost and the god and goddess emerge from within you.

WOMAN ON TOP

Being on top allows the woman more control over the depth of penetration and the rhythm and pace of movement. By adjusting the position of her hips and upper body, she can change the internal shape of her vagina and thus vary the sensations that both she and her partner feel, and she can stimulate her clitoris by rubbing it against his pubic bone.

SPOONS POSITION

In this position, you lie on your sides, knees bent, with the man behind the woman. Your bodies cup each other and, if you wish, you can make love without having to move. Lie together and breathe in unison, feeling the warmth where your bodies touch.

THE MISSIONARY

This is the basic position from which so many variations can develop. The woman lies on her back and the man enters her while lying on top of her. When the legs of both partners are stretched out straight, this position is known as the Clasping Posture. In this posture, the woman can squeeze her thigh muscles tightly together so that her vagina grips her partner's penis as it thrusts in and out.

KNEELING POSTURE

In this simple rear-entry posture, the man has both hands free to give his partner extra stimulation by caressing her and stroking her clitoris. The woman can support herself on her hands, or vary the position by taking her weight on her elbows. This posture allows deep penetration, so the man should be careful not to hurt his partner by thrusting too hard.

ELEPHANT POSTURE

This is another rear-entry position that allows deep penetration, especially when the woman puts one or more pillows under her pelvis to support herself and make it easier for her partner to enter her. As in any other lovemaking posture, the woman should always let her partner know, with gentle words or gestures, if he is thrusting too hard or if she finds the position uncomfortable.

YAB YUM POSTURE

In this comfortable and loving face-to-face posture, the man sits in a lotus position and his partner sits astride him. The name is Tibetan in origin, "Yab" meaning "father," or original male principle, and "Yum" meaning "mother," or original female principle. The posture thus represents the union of the male and female principles—cosmic oneness, the ideal resolution of all dualities (see page 129).

YAWNING POSTURE

This is a useful posture for the woman who finds it difficult to move her hips when she is making love lying on her back. By lying with her thighs raised and parted, she can vary the genital sensations for herself and her partner by, for instance, bending her knees, raising one or both legs, or crossing her legs behind her partner's back.

INDRANI POSTURE

To get into this posture, the woman lies on her back and bends both knees into her chest before her partner enters her. By bending her knees against her chest, the woman is tensing her vaginal muscles, and many women find that this tension can lead to considerable sexual arousal.

CARRIAGE POSTURE

During an active and very passionate session of lovemaking, it is wonderful to move into this posture and just lie still for a while. The man lies on one side, resting his head on one arm, with his legs straight and crossed at the ankles. His partner lies on her back at a right angle to him with her legs bent over his hips. After penetration, both partners remain still.

CHANNELING ENERGY

In the Tantric and Taoist traditions, there are specific lovemaking postures that you can use to channel energy between yourself and your partner. Making contact with different parts of each other's body increases the sexual energy, and the effects—which may be enlivening or relaxing—are felt by both of you as energy is directed from your genitals to the points where your bodies touch.

You generate relaxing and harmonizing energy during lovemaking when certain parts of your body are placed near or against those of your partner. Examples of this include holding hands, or being mouth to mouth, open eyes to open eyes, forehead to forehead, stomach to stomach, or sole of foot to sole of foot. For more stimulating energy, place different body parts against each other, such as mouth or hands to genitals, chest to feet, open eyes to closed eyes, and hands or feet to chest. By using these methods you can create whichever type of energy you desire.

ENERGY CIRCUITS

By adopting suitable positions, you and your partner can not only create energy but also enable it to flow through you both, like electricity flowing around a circuit. Using postures to channel energy brings you closer together emotionally, and when your energies merge and flow it is possible to share moments of bliss as you experience this oneness. Experiment with different postures and enjoy the sensations generated by the energy that is flowing between you.

As you move into different postures, be aware of the shapes your bodies make, where your chakras are aligned with your partner's, and how you can circulate energy by completing circuits, for instance by joining hands or mouths. One simple posture for channeling energy is for the man to sit with his legs apart, while the woman, facing him, lies on her back between his legs. She holds his feet with her hands, and he holds her feet with his hands. They do not have to move—they just look into each other's eyes and breathe together, becoming sensitive to the energy moving between them. They can hold the position for as long as they like, or until the sensations begin to fade.

The "Soixante-Neuf" or "Sixty-Nine" posture is another, more active example of one that allows both partners to complete energy circuits while generating stimulating and exciting energy.

BODY YANTRAS

Lovemaking postures in which the bodies and limbs of the two partners create harmonious shapes are also part of the Tantric tradition. These postures, like the symbolic diagrams used in meditation, are known as yantras (see page 22) and are used to channel and resonate energy. By being aware of the shapes your bodies create in particular postures, you can create your own personal yantras.

One such posture, described in the *Ananga Ranga,* is known as the Kamachakra (Wheel of Kama). In this, the man sits with his legs outstretched and parted. His partner sits facing him on his lap with her legs parted either side of him, then they hold each other's shoulders and lean backward. Their extended legs, when seen from above, resemble the spokes of a wheel. To add to this effect, they can hold hands and extend their arms out sideways, creating another pair of "spokes."

The Yab Yum Posture (see page 125) is another that creates a harmonious shape, formed by the positions of the arms and

legs of the two partners as the woman sits on the man's lap with her legs and arms wrapped around him.

YAB YUM

Yab Yum is a posture used for channeling energy. The partners stay locked in embrace and keep still, strengthened and supported by the physical union, while contemplating spiritual communion above any concern of bodily sensation. The man sits cross-legged on the floor or bed, in the lotus position, then the woman sits on his lap with her legs crossed behind his back.

MUTUAL ABSORPTION

Tantric and Taoist texts describe how partners can absorb vital essences from each other during lovemaking. To the Taoists, this mutual absorption is an exchange of Yin and Yang essences in which the man benefits from absorbing Yin essence and the woman from absorbing Yang. The potency of this exchange can be experienced only when a bond of love exists between the partners, charging the physical with the spiritual.

YIN ESSENCE

The ways in which a man can absorb Yin essence from his partner were described by a Taoist sage, Wu Hsien, in an essay written at some point during the Han Dynasty, about 2,000 years ago.

In this essay, *The Great Libation of the Three Peaks,* Wu Hsien describes three types of Yin essence—Jade Spring, White Snow, and Moon Flower Water—and explains how they can be obtained from the "Three Peaks" of a woman when she is sexually aroused. These are the top peak or Red Lotus Peak (her lips), the central peak or Twin Peaks (her nipples), and the lower peak, which he called the Dark Gate (her vulva).

JADE SPRING

Drinking Jade Spring, which is the saliva of a sexually excited woman, is considered an excellent way for a man to strengthen his Yang essence and is important for the harmony of Yin and Yang. According to Wu Hsien, Jade Spring is secreted by a pair of ducts beneath the woman's tongue, and to benefit from its special properties, the man should lick it from her Flowery Pool (her mouth) and swallow it.

WHITE SNOW

Of all the Three Peaks, the central peak, the source of White Snow, should be the first to receive attention. White Snow is the essence said to emanate from a woman's breasts during intense sexual arousal, a physical secretion that is spontaneously generated by sexual excitement and the willingness and desire of the woman to give freely. When a woman's breasts and nipples are sucked, her womb contracts and this activates her glandular system, which in turn causes the White Snow to flow. Breast secretions also occur on subtle, nonphysical levels.

White Snow, as its name suggests, is white in color, and it has a sweet taste.

When a man sucks and drinks White Snow, it will bring nourishment to his spleen and stomach. It is even more beneficial to the woman, and will improve her blood circulation, help to regularize her periods, and make her relaxed and happy. It is said to be the most potent of the three types of female sexual secretion, and that of a woman who has not produced a child is held to be particularly effective.

MOON FLOWER WATER

The highly lubricating essence found at a woman's Dark Gate during the height of sexual excitement is known as Moon Flower Water. This is normally locked away in her Palace of Yin (her womb), the gate of which will open to release the essence when the woman is approaching orgasm. The nature of the Moon Flower Water varies according to the woman's state of health, her diet, her temperament, the time of the month, and the level of sexual passion. It is considered to be at its most beneficial when its taste is sweet.

A man can absorb his partner's Moon Flower Water through his mouth, tongue, and lips during oral sex. He can also absorb it through the head of his penis during intercourse, by slightly withdrawing it from the vulva and visualizing absorption taking place. The head of the penis easily absorbs the Moon Flower Water as it flows from the womb and down the inner walls of the vagina.

Keeping the penis inside the vagina for as long as possible without ejaculation enables a man to absorb the inexhaustible supply of Yin essence from his partner. When the Moon Flower Water begins to flow, the man should withdraw his penis slightly but continue thrusting, and at the same time give his partner passionate kisses on her lips and suck her nipples.

YANG ESSENCE

If the man chooses to ejaculate and the loss of semen depletes his Yang energy and essence, he can help to counteract the loss and replenish them by consciously absorbing the woman's secretions. But a man should never force ejaculation and should avoid it if his physical body is weak. A woman is able to absorb the Yang essence of a man without him ejaculating, and it is important for both partners to understand that ejaculation is not the sole criterion for judging the act of lovemaking as successful or not. The aim is to absorb each other's essence, not to "milk" each other dry!

If a man chooses to ejaculate, or is unable to avoid it, he should enjoy it and send his semen lovingly into his partner for her to absorb, then consciously absorb her Yin essence, keeping his penis inside her vagina. Retaining semen, however, allows him to give her energy without depleting his own (see page 45).

CONGRESS OF A COW

This requires the woman to bend forward from a standing position so that she is supported on her hands and feet. Pillows, cushions, or some other form of support for her hands will reduce the amount she has to bend, and make it easier for her to maintain the posture without too much discomfort. When his partner is in position, the man approaches her from the rear and, in the words of the *Kama Sutra,* "mounts her like a bull."

ADVANCED POSTURES

These are some of the more imaginative of the postures described by the Kama Sutra. They are fun to try, and when you learn how to do them they can be exciting and satisfying. If you are unused to them, however, please note that some require strength and a good sense of balance—move very carefully to avoid damaging your muscles and spine.

THE SWING

This posture is one that really does require practice and a sense of humor while learning to master it, and also a certain amount of care to avoid the risk of back injury. The man lies on his back, then raises his body in the air, supporting himself on his feet and hands. His partner sits lightly on top of him, bends her knees to raise her legs, then gently turns her body around like a wheel on top of him while keeping his penis inside her vagina.

SPLITTING A BAMBOO

The woman first lies on her back with her legs raised while her partner kneels in front of her and enters her. Then she places one foot on her partner's shoulder and stretches the other leg out, alternating the position of her legs throughout the posture. This posture is almost a dance, and requires the woman to concentrate and feel her way to a satisfying rhythm as she alternates her leg positions.

Suspended Congress

The man stands on both feet and supports his partner by holding her buttocks, while she wraps her arms around his neck and her legs around his waist. The man may find it easier to support the weight of his partner if he bends his knees slightly, and this will also allow him to thrust more easily.

The Three Footprints

In this posture, the man stands with both feet on the ground while his partner stands, facing him, on one leg with her other leg wrapped around his waist or hooked around the back of his thigh. The man should help his partner to maintain the position, and her balance, by supporting her raised thigh with his hand. Most couples find that this is an easier posture than the Suspended Congress (left), mainly because the woman's stance is more stable but also because she can respond better to her partner's thrusting movements.

SWING-ROCKING

Both partners sit, facing each other, and put their arms around each other. After penetration, they use the weight of their bodies to create a back-and-forth rocking motion like that of a swing. This is a good posture for prolonged lovemaking.

ONE LEG UP

The woman lies on her back and the man kneels between her legs. Then she places her right leg on her partner's left shoulder while keeping her left leg on his upper thigh. After penetration, she presses against him and rocks, bringing ecstatic pleasure to both of them. This is a good posture from which to move into the Tantric Tortoise (below).

TANTRIC TORTOISE

As in the One Leg Up posture (above), the woman lies on her back and the man kneels between her legs. Then she places the soles of her feet on his chest, and after penetration he presses her knees together with his arms as he thrusts, helping her to grip his penis tightly inside her vagina.

TOTALLY AUSPICIOUS POSTURE

The partners sit or squat facing each other, and after penetration the woman leans back onto her arms and the man lifts her feet to his head. Then he places the soles of her feet first on his eyes, then on his ears, nose, mouth, and the crown of his head. This position is so named because it is supposed to bring about the granting of any desires the man may have in his mind while performing its movements.

AFTERPLAY

Lovemaking does not need to end when the man ejaculates. The mutual and combined energy that we create during lovemaking affects us all on multidimensional levels, and for both partners some gentle, loving afterplay is just as important as foreplay (see page 108).

Lovemaking, like yoga, should take time to get into and to come out of, but the natural tendency is for it to consist of an outpouring of energy, leading to orgasm and ejaculation followed by apathy and loss of interest. The man's energy is depleted after loss of semen, the woman is left feeling unfulfilled, and the lovemaking stops. Then the partners separate, rushing off to the bathroom to clean themselves without experiencing those moments of complete togetherness where both partners remain still, absorbing and experiencing the subtle energies moving in and around them.

PROLONGING THE INTIMACY

It is important to stay close together after lovemaking. This allows for the mutual exchange of subtle energies and the absorption of vital essences (see page 130). Lie together with the penis and vagina still in union and experience each other in a state of relaxation.

Enjoy the sight, smell, and taste of each other, play, talk, or laugh, and enjoy the sensations you experience in this relaxed state. Be sensitive to each other, sharing intimacy and savoring the moment.

COMMUNICATION

I think every sexually active woman knows the feelings of disappointment, and even anger, that she experiences when her man ejaculates before her sexual energy has been brought to a peak. My frustration used to result in my becoming moody and turning my back on my lover. By my very actions I was creating a distance between us, and my partner would feel guilty and disappointed, and in no way inclined to rekindle the fire.

Most men, when asked to, are willing to extend lovemaking beyond intercourse in order to satisfy their partners. After he has ejaculated, a man should be ready to give his partner further pleasuring, such as clitoral stimulation. In return, a woman should be gentle with her lover if his passion is spent before hers. And, of course, self-pleasuring can also become afterplay.

Communication is the key to true mutual satisfaction. Give each other the space to express inner feelings and desires, but the most important thing is to remain together after lovemaking for as long as you can, so that it never actually ends— you just express it in different ways.

VII

SEXUAL
HEALING

SEXUAL HEALTH

Taoism and Tantra both teach that sexual intercourse can have a very beneficial impact on health. Lovemaking, like any form of physical exercise, has a marked effect on breathing, blood circulation, heartbeat, and glandular secretions, and almost any lovemaking position can be a healing one if the intention is there.

During sex, the Yin essence of woman is brought into harmony with the Yang force of man. This harmony is healing and potentially able to put one in communion with the infinite forces of nature. Sexual intercourse also directs healing energy to the body's vital organs by stimulating the reflexology points of the genitals (see opposite).

There are two major factors that allow healing to take place. The first is body position and its effect on the internal organs. Body position also affects the shape of the vagina, which is extremely important because different postures gently mold the vagina into different shapes. These determine which of its reflexology zones are stimulated by the penis, and which zones of the penis are stimulated by the vagina.

The second factor that promotes healing is the intention of both partners, one as the "healer" and the other as the "receiver."

> **"Without harmony of Yin and Yang, neither medicines nor aphrodisiacs will be of any use."**
>
> THE PLAIN GIRL

Healing is effected through the energy generated. Using the postures shown on the following pages as a guide, both partners should focus on their breathing and use their minds to channel energy to the various organs or parts of the body that are in need of healing. Quiet your minds and use your breath to guide the energy. Breathing, yoga, and meditation will help you to become more sensitive to energy moving inside your bodies.

When engaging in healing postures for the man's sake, the woman also benefits because her partner is thrusting along her vaginal reflexology zones and she is receiving general sexual pleasure. With the healing postures for women, the man should vary the depth of penetration to massage the required part of the vagina. As the healer, he should experience the pleasure of serving his partner—very much in the spirit of the Tao of loving.

You should not, of course, rely solely on the effects of these healing postures to cure or relieve an illness or injury—you must always consult a physician first.

Healing Techniques

When intercourse is intended to help ease a man's problem, just assuming a sexual position is not enough to effect healing. That also needs careful control of penile thrusting and ejaculation, and an even stimulation of the entire penis to direct energy to the internal organs. Factors that contribute to the success of a position for a woman are whether the vagina changes shape to make a particular area more accessible, if the penis comes into contact with the appropriate zone of the vagina, and the amount and nature of penile thrusting; ejaculation is to be avoided.

These healing techniques have been used for thousands of years. To gain the utmost benefit from them, dedication, time to honor the practices and, most importantly, a loving attitude are required.

Sexual Reflexology

Energy runs through the body along meridians (channels) that are linked to the internal organs. Reflexology (see page 86) teaches that points on the feet, hands, and ears correspond to certain major meridians, and massaging these points can relieve internal problems.

Similarly, the shaft and head of the penis and areas along the vaginal passage can be divided into zones, each of which is allied to a major internal organ. During lovemaking, stimulation of the reflexology zones of the penis and vagina will send healing energy to the corresponding internal organs, for example, from the heart zone to the heart and from the lung zone to the lungs.

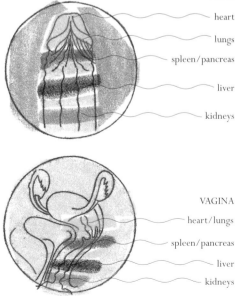

PENIS
heart
lungs
spleen/pancreas
liver
kidneys

VAGINA
heart/lungs
spleen/pancreas
liver
kidneys

REFLEXOLOGY ZONES
The principal reflexology zones of the male and female genitalia connect with the heart, lungs, spleen, pancreas, liver, and kidneys. Most of the genital reflexology zones can be stimulated by masturbation, but more effective stimulation can be achieved by making love, especially in one of the healing postures described on the following pages.

HEALING POSTURES

I have based the following postures for healing specific ailments on those recommended by Dr. Stephen Chang in his book The Tao of Sexology, *but almost any lovemaking position can be a healing one if the intention is there. If you decide to make love with your partner in order to ease a particular problem that one or both of you may have, then provided you both approach it with a loving attitude, healing is what will happen. For general healing purposes, you can use any of your favorite postures combined with four or five Sets of Nine (see page 120).*

DRAGON POSTURE

This is good therapy for erection problems and premature ejaculation. The woman lies on her side, hips facing upward as far as possible, and the man enters from above. It is quite a difficult posture for the man, but two Sets of Nine each day in this posture will bring improvement in 15 days.

PHOENIX POSTURE

This whole-body healing posture promotes a man's overall physical health, and it is recommended that it be repeated nine times a day for ten days, utilizing up to nine Sets of Nine. The woman starts out on her knees, then gently bends all the way back until her head and back are as flat as possible (the more flexible she is, the farther back she'll be able to bend). One or more pillows placed under her back will make the posture more comfortable for her. The man enters her from above, and supports his weight on his hands.

UNICORN POSTURE

This variation of the Missionary Position (see page 123) is energizing for the man and also benefits the woman by creating a partial vacuum in her vagina, which will stimulate certain of her internal organs. The woman lies on her back, thighs raised and parted, with her head and shoulders supported by pillows, then her partner lies between her legs and penetrates her. Practicing three Sets of Nine three times a day in this posture will completely energize a man's body in 20 days.

SWAN POSTURE

This is a whole-body
energizing posture for
women who suffer
from energy blockages
resulting in headaches,
poor blood circulation,
and menstrual prob-
lems including cramps
and abnormally heavy
or low flow. The
woman must hold her
partner's penis,
because penetration
is difficult in this
position, and then she
should rotate her
pelvis for as long as she
comfortably can.

FLAMINGO POSTURE

When the woman lies on her left with left leg bent, and her partner performs five Sets of Nine up to five times a day for ten days, this posture aids arthritis and bone problems. When she lies on her right with right leg bent, and he performs six Sets of Nine, six times a day for 20 days, it helps with blood vessel problems.

SWALLOW POSTURE

This is good for relieving anemia and poor blood circulation. The woman lies on her back with her knees bent into her chest and her feet in the air, then the man kneels in front of her and penetrates deeply. The position of the woman's body when in this posture shortens her vagina, allowing deep penetration, and she should rotate her pelvis while her partner keeps still.

TURTLE POSTURE

In this general healing posture, the woman lies on her back with her knees bent into her chest. The man enters from the front and uses his partner's legs to rub her breasts while she does the moving. The movements of this legs-bent-into-the-chest position massage the woman's intestines, causing energy to flow to them.

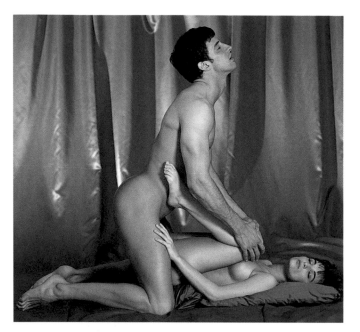

KINGFISHER POSTURE

This posture has a beneficial effect on the woman's reproductive organs, and also helps to relieve problems arising from the stomach and spleen, particularly digestive problems. The woman lies on her back, suported by pillows, if necessary, with her legs wrapped around the man's waist. He supports himself on his hands and knees and enters her, penetrating shallowly. Then she rotates her pelvis alternately clockwise and counterclockwise for as long as possible.

DOVE POSTURE

The woman lies on her back and wraps her legs around the man's thighs, while he kneels and penetrates with no more than the head and first two inches of his penis. After her partner has penetrated her, the woman rotates her pelvis alternately clockwise and counterclockwise for as long as she can. This posture helps to relieve problems related to the pancreas and liver and alleviates weakness of the knees and other joints.

SNAKE POSTURE

In this posture, the way that the man and woman move will determine the benefits that are to be gained. If he has blood problems, such as low blood pressure or anemia, he can relieve them by moving up and down under her, making seven Sets of Nine up to seven times a day for ten days. Eight Sets of Nine, eight times a day for 15 days, will help him with lymphatic problems. If he lies still and his partner moves up and down on his penis while rotating her pelvis, her vagina will be thoroughly massaged and her nervous system, liver, and eyesight will benefit.

MONKEY POSTURE

This is particularly helpful for water retention problems, but it is hard for the woman to do. The man lies on his back and the woman kneels, facing his feet. She holds her partner's penis, allowing only the head to enter, while rotating her pelvis alternately clockwise and counterclockwise.

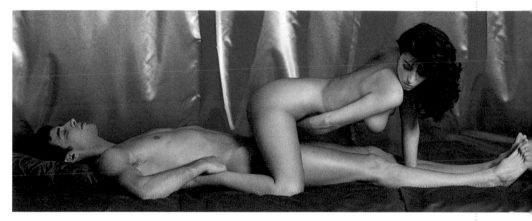

RABBIT POSTURE

This posture is beneficial for a woman who is suffering from a lack of energy leading to faintness and weak breathing. The woman lies on her back, and, as in the Missionary Position, the man lies on top and enters deeply. Then the woman simply rotates her pelvis alternately clockwise and counterclockwise. Although she may experience orgasm when making love like this, it is not the aim of the posture, but it will add to the overall healing benefits.

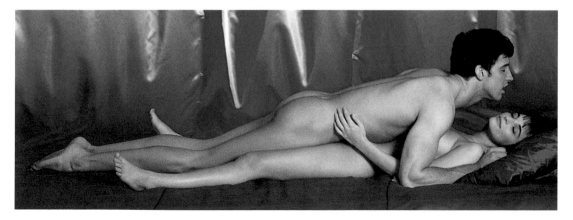

Soft-style Lovemaking

There are always those times when one or neither of you feels like making love, yet you long to share intimacy with your partner. Soft-style lovemaking can be penetrative or nonpenetrative, and the emphasis is on relaxation, emotional intimacy, and harmony. There is no goal to be attained: it involves simply being together and appreciating that making love doesn't always have to involve penetrative sex or an erect penis.

Sometimes the desire we have to be touched, caressed, and held is misinterpreted as a need to have sex, when very often just being physically close to someone is all that is really wanted. The energy exchange between two people simply holding each other can be as satisfying and fulfilling as penetrative sex, and lying naked with someone has its own magic. This magic derives from many factors, such as the shape of each other's body, the sensation of breath on the skin, the smell of each other, and the feel of each other.

Foreplay is generally considered to be the "play" leading up to sexual intercourse, which means that it is often rushed and the appreciation, awe, and wonder of just being together is lost as we race toward the climax of genital union.

A common problem for couples in long-term relationships is that much of the initial excitement and adventure has gone because they know each other so well, they skimp on foreplay or perform it without savoring the experience, and they get used to making love in the same way, time after time. It becomes repetitive and boring, because they have lost sight (and touch, smell, and taste) of each other's true sexual attraction. A particular touch, gesture, or other action becomes a signal for the desire to make love, and then the familiar pattern emerges—tried, tested, and often unsatisfying for both partners.

Reinventing sex

There are all kinds of ways to "reinvent" sex for ourselves, for instance by introducing a playful element to our lovemaking: as adults, we very often forget the necessity and importance of aspects of play. There are also great rewards to be gained from making love in a peaceful, gentle, and relaxed way.

Sexual gymnastics are not for everyone all the time, and there can be much pleasure to be had in, for example, simply lying still together in the Spoons Position (see page 122), with or without penetration. Just lie still, embracing each other and breathing together for a few minutes, and then change sides.

Love puja is a form of nonpenetrative sex that allows you to make love with your partner without any physical sexual contact. Sit facing your partner, place your left hand on his or her heart center, and cover his or her left hand with your right hand. Look into each other's left eye and breathe together. Receive energy and love from each other as you inhale, and give to each other as you exhale.

This is a method of harmonizing and balancing your energy, and the simplicity of the practice gives it the power to connect you in a deep, heart-felt way with your partner and with yourself.

SOFT-ENTRY SEX

Sometimes, when a couple want penetrative sex, the man is unable to achieve an erection. But this need not prevent them from having intercourse, because penetration is possible without an erection. It may require a little practice and careful handling, but by using his fingers (and a lubricant, if necessary), a man can gently insert at least part of his penis into his partner's vagina.

Then, if he uses his forefinger and thumb to form a ring gripping the base of his penis, the pressure will help to retain the blood in the end of his penis, making it semi-rigid and enabling him to thrust gently. Eventually, he might find that he has a full erection. Entry is easier if you lie on your sides in the Spoons Position or facing each other, or with the man on top.

Soft-entry sex can be used by a man to re-enter his partner and regain his erection if he has wholly or partially lost it while practicing semen retention (see page 46). It also gives both partners the opportunity to practice genital muscle control. Alternatively, after penetration has been achieved, they can find a comfortable position for both to lie in and just keep still, visualizing the energy circulating between them and letting their breathing patterns align naturally with one another.

For most women, feeling a man grow hard inside them is an erotic sensation. But if an erection doesn't happen, it need not matter, because a woman can enjoy the experience for what it is, and use it to harmonize her physical, mental, and emotional energies with her partner's.

SEXUAL ABSTINENCE

When a couple indulge in a short period of voluntary sexual abstinence, it not only encourages sexual feelings and erotic sentiments for one another but it also helps them to concentrate and focus their sexual energy, increases their sensitivity, and strengthens their bodies. A program of yoga (see page 48), including a healthy diet and breathing practice, is helpful during times of abstinence, because it keeps the vital energy moving in the body.

Sexual abstinence can have the effect of heightening your sensitivity and stimulating your desire—you always want what you can't have.

SAFER SEX

Sex is one of the great pleasures in life and vital to our existence as a species. Let's keep it pleasurable and a source of ecstasy by keeping it safe—a thin sheath of rubber will in no way diminish your pleasure and enjoyment if you are sharing love with your partner.

The purpose of so-called "safer sex" is to minimize the risk of a sexually transmitted disease (STD) being passed from one partner to the other. Practicing safer sex is especially important at the beginning of a relationship, while you are still learning about each other's sexual history and cannot be reasonably certain that there is no risk of infecting each other.

Safer sex techniques include the use of condoms to prevent infection by exchange of bodily fluids (such as semen, blood, and vaginal secretions) during intercourse, and a number of nonpenetrative forms of love-making. These include, for example, erotic embracing, stroking, and massage, and mutual self-pleasuring in which you avoid direct contact with each other's bodily fluids.

The main reason for avoiding contact with each other's bodily fluids is that these can carry the viruses responsible for infections such as syphilis and hepatitis B, as well as the Human Immunodeficiency Virus (HIV) that causes Acquired Immune Deficiency Syndrome (AIDS).

We know that sexually transmitted diseases are a potential threat to anyone who has sex, and their effects are damaging physically, mentally, and emotionally and potentially life-threatening. Do not rely on anyone but yourself to protect you from STDs. Take proper responsibility for your own health and determine your own standards of safety, but remember that it is not enough to rely on a positive mental attitude to save you from the threat of disease. Don't risk your health and life—that is not Tantra or the way of the Tao.

This does not mean that you have to become celibate: just question yourself about your attitudes to the issues of sexuality, use your intelligence, and respect and honor the temple of the body. If you respect yourself and respect your partner there should be no question or doubt as to whether or not to use a condom.

NEW RELATIONSHIPS

Very often, however, the first time you make love with someone there is a feeling of tension and awkwardness. But anyone who has difficulty in broaching the subject of safer sex with a prospective partner obviously does not know him or her well enough to be contemplating penetrative sex. It may be difficult, but it is often more sensible to wait until you know each other better than to begin having sex too soon—especially unprotected sex—and you miss the pleasure of the journey if you race to your destination.

The pleasure, in this case, is that of getting to know your partner properly in advance, through honest communication, through touch, and by building an intimacy and trust that prepares your bodies and minds for intercourse. It also gives you the chance to experiment with non-penetrative sex to discover how sexual pleasure can be a whole-body experience, rather than just a genital sensation.

Extended foreplay can be as arousing and stimulating as intercourse. It is a delightful and erotic way of getting to know someone and assessing your compatibility. But avoid oral sex with a first-time partner. Instead, use a lubricant (such as K-Y Jelly) and experiment with giving him or her genital stimulation using an inventive range of hand and finger strokes.

ESTABLISHED RELATIONSHIPS

For long-term partners who are monogamous, using nonpenetrative sex methods (whether as extended foreplay or as an alternative to intercourse) will enhance your relationship and your sexuality, and deepen your mutual feelings of trust, love, and intimacy. This will make it easier for you to communicate honestly and openly, and to share your innermost feelings and

develop a clear understanding of each other. Combined with sensitivity and awareness, this in turn will strengthen your relationship and increase your potential for the ecstasy of divine union, elevating your love to a new dimension.

Both Tantrism and Taoism stress the importance of the male and female in balanced and harmonious union, the divine union of two separate yet complementary forces. These philosophies are not, of course, just about sex, but they incorporate it into everyday life in a way that brings health, happiness, and liberation.

TOUCH AND INTIMACY
Use touch and intimacy to help you get to know each other properly.

GLOSSARY

A

AGAMAS Ancient texts on practical and theoretical *yoga* and *Tantra*

AJNA The brow *chakra*

ANAHATA The heart *chakra*

ANANDA Supreme or spiritual bliss

APANA One of the forms of *prana*

ASANAS The postures of *yoga*

ATMAN The inner self, or soul

AUM A variant spelling of *Om*

B

BANDHA A *yoga* posture involving muscular contractions, or "locks"

BHAKTI Self-denying devotional surrender

BINDU The dot at the centre of a *yantra*, representing the male seed and the Supreme Consciousness

BRAHMA The Creator, one of the three aspects (along with *Vishnu* and *Shiva*) of the Supreme Being

C

CHAKRAS The energy centers in the *subtle body* that connect it with the physical body

CHI The Taoist term for *subtle energy*

CHING The Taoist term for sexual energy

COSMIC BODY The cosmos visualized as a human body

D

DAKINI In Tantric Buddhism, a spiritually endowed woman who passes on divine knowledge through sexual intercourse

DEVI The Mother Goddess, one of the forms of *Shakti*

A Nepalese painting depicting the lower chakras as flowers.

F

FOUR HOLY TRUTHS The basic teachings that were expounded in the Buddha's first sermon

G

GUNAS The three fundamental forms of energy: *Sattva, Rajas,* and *Tamas*

H

HATHA YOGA One of the forms of *yoga* that involve physical postures

HATHA YOGA PRADIPIKA A medieval text describing the philosophy and practice of Hatha Yoga, written by Yogi Swami Svatmarama

I

I CHING The "Book of Changes," an ancient Chinese book containing guidance on predicting future events

IDA One of the subtle body's three major *nadis,* or energy channels

J

JALANDHARA BANDHA A *bandha* that is used to prevent *prana* escaping from the upper body

K

KALACHAKRA The Wheel of Time, a Tantric Buddhist practice involving meditation and *mandalas*

KALI One of the principal forms of *Devi,* the Mother Goddess

KAMA The Hindu god of love; the personification of love

KUNDALINI The powerful, normally latent female energy, usually depicted as a coiled serpent, that is located in the base *chakra*

L

LINGAM The penis, or a symbolic representation of it as an emblem of *Shiva*

M

MAHAKALA Great Time, one of the forms of *Shiva*

MAHARAGA The highest form of passion

MAHAVIDYAS Ten forms of *Devi,* the Mother Goddess, that each represent a different dimension of knowledge

MAHESHWARA The Great Lord, or Lord of Creation, one of the forms of *Shiva*

MANDALA A mystical circular diagram used in *meditation* to concentrate cosmic and psychic energy

MANTRA A syllable or phrase that is

repeated either out loud or silently as an aid to *meditation*

MAYA Illusion or Deception, one of the forms of *Shakti*

MEDITATION Stilling the mind and focusing it on an image or symbol, such as a *yantra,* to produce an inner tranquility that brings spiritual nourishment

MOKSHA The state of liberation from delusion and suffering

MUDRA A hand gesture used in *meditation* to channel subtle energy

MULA BANDHA A *bandha* that is used to prevent *apana* escaping from the lower body and to stimulate the base *chakra*

MULADHARA The base *chakra*

N

NADA The male and female energies (*Shiva* and *Shakti*) manifested as sound

NADIS Channels in the *subtle body* through which *subtle energy* flows

O

OM The most powerful of all *mantras,* said to be the original sound from which the universe was created

P

PADMA The lotus flower

PARVATI The Mountaineer, one of the forms of *Shakti*

PINGALA One of the *subtle body*'s three major *nadis,* or energy channels

PRAKRITI The material world, the manifestation of *Maya*

PRANA One of the forms of *subtle energy* that flow within the *subtle body*

PRANAYAMA The branch of *yoga* that is concerned with breath control and breathing exercises

PUJA Ritual and worship

PURANAS Sanskrit writings celebrating the actions and powers of the gods

R

RAGA Passion

RAJAS One of the three *Gunas:* the energy of activity and motion

S

SAHASRARA The crown *chakra*

SAMANA One of the forms of *prana*

SANSKRIT The language of the Hindu scriptures and other texts. It is an ancient member of the vast Indo-European language family, which includes Hindi and English

SATTVA One of the three *Gunas:* the energy of clarity and truth

SHAKTI: The Supreme Goddess, consort of *Shiva;* the female principle or energy

SHIVA The Destroyer, one of the three aspects (along with *Brahma* and *Vishnu*) of the Supreme Being. Consort of *Shakti;* the male principle or energy

SUBTLE BODY The nonphysical body that surrounds and permeates the physical body, and is believed to connect this world with the next

SUBTLE ENERGY The energy that flows through the *nadis* in the *subtle body*

SUSHUMNA The most important of the *subtle body*'s three major *nadis,* or energy channels

SUTRA A spiritual text, discourse, or aphorism

T

TAMAS One of the three *Gunas:* the energy of solidity and inertia

TANKA A Tibetan iconic painting

TANTRA A philosophy and way of life that includes using sexual energy to achieve liberation from the limitations of the self

TAOISM An ancient system of living and body of knowledge that originated in China. It teaches adherence to the way of the creative principle that orders the universe, and was expounded in texts such as the "Tao Te Ching" of Lao Tzu and the writings of Chuang Tzu

TRATAKA Gazing at a candle to develop concentration and strengthen the eyes

U

UDANA One of the forms of *prana*

UDDIYANA BANDHA A *bandha* that gives support to the lungs and balances various elements in the body

V

VISHNU The Preserver, one of the three aspects (along with *Brahma* and *Shiva*) of the Supreme Being

VYANA One of the forms of *prana*

Y

YANTRA A mystical diagram (often the visual representation of a *mantra*) that is used in *meditation*

YIN AND YANG In Taoism, the Cosmic Feminine is known as Yin and the Cosmic Masculine as Yang. The constant interplay between these two opposites makes up the entire universe

YOGA A system of exercises that promote physical and mental well-being and can facilitate the union of the individual self with pure consciousness

YONI The vulva, or a symbolic representation of it as an emblem of *Shakti*

Z

ZEN A Japanese form of Buddhism that seeks enlightenment by intuition through *meditation*

INDEX

A

Absorption, mutual 130

Abstinence, sexual 151

Afterplay 138

Alternate nostril breathing 17
exercises 56

Anuloma viloma 17

Anus
female 28
male 38

Ananga Ranga
on erogenous zones 30
on genital size and shape 42
on Kamachakra posture 129

Apana 17

Arousal
during foreplay 108
female 29
male 39

Asanas 58

Auras 16

B

Bandhas 55
Jalandhara 55
Mula 55
Uddiyana 55

Bathing 101
and massage 93
fire 101
mud 101
sun 101

The Swing (see page 133).

Bindu 23

Bladder
female 28
male 38

Book of Changes 15

Brahma 14

Body ornamentation 98

Breath control 54
and bandhas 55
during meditation 85
during yoga 59
techniques 54
to control ejaculation 46

C

Candlelight
for bathing 101
for massage 103
in sacred space 100

Candles
for meditation 85

Cervix 28

Chakras 18
and meditation 85
attributes 19
base (muladhara) 19
and Shakti 14
brow (ajna) 19
and Shiva 14
discovering 18
heart (anahata) 19
positions 18
resident deities 14
sacral (svadisthana) 19
solar plexus (manipura) 19
throat (vishuddi) 19
visualization 18

Channeling energy 128

Chi 16
and Yin and Yang 15

Chi Po 115

Chinese medicine 15

Ching 16

Classic of the Plain Girl 13

Clitoris 28

Communication 138

Cosmic Feminine 15

Cosmic Masculine 15

Creativity 93

D

Dance of Shiva and Shakti 14

Dancing 99

Deities within 96

Devi 14

Diet 50

Durga 14

E

Eating 53

Ejaculation
female 35
male 44

Ejaculation control
and orgasm 44
importance of 26
semen retention 45
techniques 46

Elements
air 90
akasa 90
and chakras 19

earth 88
fire 89
sex and 88
water 89

ENERGIES 16
chi 15
ching 16
kundalini 20
sexual 17

ENERGY
channelling 128
circuits 128

EPIDIDYMIS 38

EROGENOUS ZONES
female 30
male 40

EROTIC DANCING 99

ESSENTIAL OILS
for bathing 101
for massage 103
in sacred space 100
to scent a room 102

EXERCISE 48

F

FEMALE PARTNER 28

FEMININE ASPECTS 27

FITNESS 58

FOOD 50
eating 53
preparation 52
Rajasic 52
Sattvic 51
Tamasic 53
types of 50

FORBIDDENS, THE 114
emotions 115
energy loss 114

external energy 114
food, drink, and drugs 115
water 115

FOREPLAY 108

G

GAMES 90

GAURI 14

GENITALS
female 28
male 38

GLANS 38

GODDESS OF THE SHELL 120

GREAT LIBATION OF THE THREE PEAKS **130**

G-SPOT 29
stimulation of 29

GUNAS 51
symbolized in yantras 23

H I J

HATHA YOGA 48

HEALING POSTURES 142

HEALING TECHNIQUES 141

HEALTH, SEXUAL 140

HOMOSEXUALITY 116

HSÜAN NÜ 13

HUANG TI 13

HUANG TI NEI CHING **115**

I CHING **15**

IDA 17

ILLUSION, VEIL OF 14

INCENSE
in bathroom 101
in massage room 103
in sacred space 100

INNER MAN 27

INNER WOMAN 27

INNER SMILE 85

JADE SPRING 130
drinking 111

K

KALI 14

KAMACHAKRA POSTURE 129

KAMA SUTRA
author of 119
on fellatio 112
on genital size and shape 42
on kissing 111
on lovemaking postures 119
on movements of
the man 121
on PC muscle control 33

KIRLIAN PHOTOGRAPHY 16

KISSING 110
techniques 110
types of 110

KUNDALINI 20
awakening 20

KUNDALINI SHAKTI 20

L

LABIA 28

LAO TZU 13

LINGAM 14

LOTUS POSTURE 85

LOVEMAKING
endless 44
enhanced 33
movements 120
rituals 94

soft-style 150

LOVEMAKING POSTURES 118
Advanced 133
Congress of a Cow 132
One Leg Up 136
Splitting a Bamboo 133
Suspended Congress 134
Swing 133
Swing-rocking 135
Tantric Tortoise 136
Three Footprints 134
Totally Auspicious 137

Healing 142
Dove 147
Dragon 142
Flamingo 145
Kingfisher 146
Monkey 149
Phoenix 142
Rabbit 149
Snake 148
Swallow 145
Swan 144
Turtle 146
Unicorn 143

Old Favorites 119
Carriage 127
Elephant 124
Indrani 127
Kneeling 124
Missionary 123
Spoons 122
Woman on Top 122
Yab Yum 125
energy channeling 129
Yawning 126

LOVE PUJA 151

M

MALE PARTNER 38

MANDALAS 24
and meditation 24

MANTRAS 21
and meditation 21

of chakras 19

MARE'S POSITION 33

MASCULINE ASPECTS 27

MASSAGE, SENSUAL 102
  and bathing 93
  and touch 102
  arms and hands 107
  back 106
  buttocks 106
  feet 107
  finishing 107
  front 106
  giving and receiving 106
  head and face 107
  legs 106
  shoulders 106

MASSAGE OILS 103
  blending 103

MASSAGE STROKES
  Feathering 105
  Gliding 104
  Knuckling 105
  Percussion 105

MAYA 14

MEDITATION 84
  exercises 85
    inner smile 85
    using a candle 85
  using mandalas 24
  using mantras 21

MENSTRUAL CYCLE 36

MENSTRUATION 36
  attitudes to 37
  rituals 37

MOON FLOWER WATER 131

MOTHER GODDESS 14

Lovemaking in 17th-century India.

MUDRA 85

MUSCLE CONTROL 26

MUTUAL ABSORPTION 130

MYSTERIOUS GIRL, THE 13

N

NADIS 17
  and chakras 16

NINE MOVEMENTS OF THE MAN 121

NINE SHALLOW, ONE DEEP 120

O

OM (MANTRA) 21

ORAL SEX 112
  cunnilingus 113
  fellatio 112
  tongue exercises 112

ORGASM, FEMALE 34
  and arousal 29
  clitoral and vaginal 35
  Nine Levels of 35

ORGASM, MALE 44
  and arousal 39
  and ejaculation 44

OVARIES
  and menstrual cycle 36
  position of 28

P

PADMASANA 85

PC (PUBOCOCCYGEAL) MUSCLE
  female 32
    exercising 32

  using 43
  male 43
    exercising 43
    using 43

PENIS 38
  anatomy 38
  exercises for 42
  size and shape 42

PINGALA 17

PLAIN GIRL, THE 13
  on the stages of loving 121

PRANA 16
  flow of 17

PRANAYAMA YOGA 54

PROSTATE GLAND 38
  stimulation of 39

PUBIC BONE
  female 28
  male 38

R

RAINBOW GIRL, THE 13

RAJAS 51

RAJASIC FOODS 52

REFLEXOLOGY 86
  zones 87
    feet 87
    penis 141
    vagina 141

RELATIONSHIPS 153

RELAXATION
  and lovemaking 83
  techniques 83

REST AND RENEWAL 82

RITUALS, LOVEMAKING 94

RHYTHMS OF LOVE 120

ROLE REVERSAL 97

S

SACRED SPACE 100

SAFER SEX 152

SATISFACTION, MUTUAL 34

SATTVA 51

SATTVIC FOODS 51

SCROTUM 38

SELF EXAMINATION, FEMALE 29

SELF PLEASURING, MALE 41

SEMINAL VESICLE 38

SEMEN
production of 39
retention 45
techniques 46

SENSES, AWAKENING 88
playful games 90

SETS OF NINE 120

SETTING THE SCENE 92
preparing your bodies 93

SEXUAL ANATOMY
female 28
male 38

SEXUAL HEALTH 140
healing techniques 141

SEXUAL REFLEXOLOGY 141

SEXUALITY, EXPLORING 26

SHAKTI 14
in ritual lovemaking 95

SHIVA 14
in ritual lovemaking 95

SLEEP 80

SOFT-STYLE LOVEMAKING 150

STRESS 82

SU NÜ 13

SU NÜ CHING 13

SUBTLE BODY 16

SUPREME BEING 14

SUPREME SOURCE 15

SUSHUMNA 17

T

TAMAS 51

TAMASIC FOODS 53

TANTRISM 12

TAOISM 12

TAO TE CHING 13

TESTICLES 38

TONGUE EXERCISES 112

TOUCH 102

TENSION 82

TSAI NÜ 13

U V W

UMA 14

URETHRA
female 28
male 38

URETHRAL SPONGE 29
and female ejaculation 35

UTERUS 28

VAGINA 28

VAS DEFERENS 38

VATSYAYANA 119

VISHNU 14

VISUALIZATION OF CHAKRAS 18

VITAL AIRS 17

WHEEL OF KAMA POSTURE 129

WHITE SNOW 130

WU HSIEN 130

Y

YAB YUM 125
for channeling energy 129

YANG
and Yin 15
essence 131
energy 27
and homosexuality 116
nature of 15

YANTRAS 22
body 129
Kali 23
Tara 22

YELLOW EMPEROR, THE 13

YELLOW EMPEROR'S CLASSIC
OF INTERNAL MEDICINE 115

YIN
and Yang 15
essence 130
energy 27
and homosexuality 116
nature of 15

YIN/YANG SYMBOL 15
as a mandala 24

YOGA 48
and sex 49
benefits of 48
face, jaw, and eye
exercises 79
for two 59
neck and head exercises 76
practice 49
precautions 59
tips for practising 59

YOGA POSTURES
Bridge 74
Butterfly 61
Camel 73
Chest Opener 68
Child's Posture 73
Cobra 65
Corpse 61
Dog Posture 67
Fish 66
Forward Bends 63
Goddess 60
Headstand 70
Supported 71
Inclined Plane 63
Kneeling 72
Leg raises 64
Pelvic Bounces 62
Pelvic Thrusts 72
Shoulder Exercise 66
Shoulderstand and Plow 75
Sidestretch 69
Single-leg Forward Bends 62
Surrender 60

YONI 14

FURTHER READING

ANAND, MARGO. *The Art of Sexual Ecstasy.* Los Angeles: Jeremey P. Tarcher, Inc., 1989.

CHANG, DR. STEPHEN T. *The Best Way to Make Love Work.* San Francisco: Tao Publishing, 1986.

CHANG, JOLAN. *The Tao of Love and Sex: The Ancient Chinese Way to Ecstasy.* New York: Viking Penguin, 1991.

CHIA, MANTAK. *Awaken Healing Energy Through The Tao.* Santa Fe, New Mexico: Aurora Press, 1983.

CHIA, MANTAK AND CHIA, MANEEWAN. *Awaken Healing Light of Tao.* Huntington, New York: Healing Tao Books, 1993.

CHIA, MANTAK, AND CHIA, MANEEWAN. *Healing Love through the Tao: Cultivating Female Sexual Energy.* Huntington, New York: Healing Tao Books, 1986.

CHIA, MANTAK AND WINN, MICHAEL. *Taoist Secrets of Love: Cultivating Male Sexual Energy.* Santa Fe, New Mexico: Aurora Press, 1984.

COPONY, HEITA. *Mystery of Mandalas.* Wheaton, Illinois: Theosophical Publishing House, 1989.

DOUGLAS, NIK, AND SLINGER, PENNY. *Sexual Secrets: The Alchemy of Ecstasy.* Rochester, Vermont: Destiny Books, 1979.

GIA-FU FENG AND ENGLISH, JANE (trans.). *Tao Te Ching.* Hampshire, England: Wildwood House, 1973.

GREY, ALEX, WILBER, KEN, AND McCORMICK, CARLO. *Sacred Mirrors: The Visionary Art of Alex Grey.* Rochester, Vermont: Inner Traditions International, 1990.

GRIGG, RAY. *The Tao of Relationships.* Atlanta, Georgia: Humanics, Ltd., 1992.

HAY, LOUISE L. *You Can Heal Your Life.* Carson, California: Hay House, 1987.

JOHARI, HARISH. *Tools for Tantra.* Rochester, Vermont: Destiny Books, 1986.

JUDITH, ANODEA. *Wheels of Life.* Saint Paul, Minnesota: Llewellyn Publications, 1990.

LAWLOR, ROBERT. *Earth Honoring the New Male Sexuality.* Rochester, Vermont: Inner Traditions International, 1989.

MOOKERJI, AJIT. *Kali: The Feminine Force.* London: Thames and Hudson, 1983.

MOOKERJI, AJIT. *Kundalini: The Arousal of the Inner Energy.* London: Thames and Hudson, 1982.

MOOKERJEE, AJIT, AND KHANNA, MADHU. *The Tantric Way: Art, Science, Ritual.* London: Thames and Hudson Ltd., 1977.

RAJNEESH, BHAGWAN SHREE. *Tantra, Spirituality and Sex.* Oregon: Rajneesh Foundation International, 1977.

RAJNEESH, BHAGWAN SHREE. *Tantra: The Supreme Understanding.* Oregon: Rajneesh Foundation International, 1977.

RAJNEESH, OSHO. *From Sex to Super-Consciousness.* Cologne, Germany: The Rebel Publishing House, 1979.

RAWSON, PHILIP. *Tantra: The Indian Cult of Ecstasy.* New York: Thames and Hudson, 1989.

SIVANANDA YOGA CENTRE, THE. *The Book of Yoga.* London: Ebury Press, 1983.

TANSLEY, DAVID V. *Subtle Body: Essence and Shadow.* New York: Thames and Hudson, 1989.

ACKNOWLEDGMENTS

Illustrators:
Jane Craddock-Watson: 3, 6, 7, 8, 14, 19, 20, 22, 23, 35, 119, 121, 141 (top)

Lesli Sternberg: 17, 18, 28, 30, 31, 32, 36, 38, 39, 40, 41, 43, 86, 99, 141 (bottom)

Paul Williams: 11, 25, 47, 81, 91, 117, 139

Picture credits:
Charles Walker Collection/Images (Colour Library): 24, 154; Fitzwilliam Museum, University of Cambridge/Bridgeman Art Library, London: 33, 158; Photo Scala, Florence: 129; Private Collection/Bridgeman Art Library: 109; Victor Lownes Collection/Bridgeman Art Library, London: 156; Werner Forman Archive: 113.

Production consultant:
Lorraine Baird

Text input:
Maddalena Bastianelli

Picture research:
Sandra Schneider